America

Theory Redux series
Series editor: Laurent de Sutter

Published Titles

America

The Troubled Continent
of Thought

Avital Ronell

polity

The publisher gratefully acknowledges permission to reproduce the following copyright material: Avital Ronell, "The *Gestell* from Hell: Philosophy Sets Up 'America,'" *Oxford Literary Review*, 43.1, 2021 (special issue "A Conversation with Jacques Derrida about Heidegger," edited by Rodrigo Therezo and Geoffrey Bennington), pp. 107–131.

First published in 2024 by Polity Press

Polity Press
65 Bridge Street
Cambridge CB2 1UR, UK

Polity Press
111 River Street
Hoboken, NJ 07030, USA

ISBN-13: 978-1-5095-6026-4
ISBN-13: 978-1-5095-6027-1(pb)

A catalogue record for this book is available from the British Library.

Library of Congress Control Number: 2024932609

Typeset in 12.5 on 15pt Adobe Garamond
by Cheshire Typesetting Ltd, Cuddington, Cheshire
Printed and bound in Great Britain by TJ Books Ltd, Padstow, Cornwall

For further information on Polity, visit our website:
politybooks.com

For Pierre Alferi, on the road again.

Contents

I once raised the question, with respect to
Thoreau, whether America has expressed
itself philosophically.

Stanley Cavell[1]

I became insane, with long
intervals of horrible sanity.

Edgar Allen Poe[2]

I'm Nobody! Who are you?

Emily Dickinson[3]

[1] Stanley Cavell, "Finding as Founding: Taking Steps in Emerson's 'Experience,'" in Stanley Cavell and David Justin Hodge (eds.), *Emerson's Transcendental Etudes* (Stanford, CA: Stanford University Press, 2003).

[2] Edgar Allan Poe to George Washington Eveleth, January 4, 1848 (LTR-259), Edgar Allan Poe Society of Baltimore. https://www.eapoe.org/works/letters/p4801040.htm.

[3] *The Poems of Emily Dickinson: Reading Edition*, edited by R. W. Franklin (Cambridge, MA: Harvard University Press, 1998).

1

Unfriending the Gods

Among so many time-release questions and effects of language, we are given to understand that events turning on historical delivery still hit you in the gut and make your immune system give way – and not only because of this or that decimating decree, violent dispatch, or throwback to primal injury. Friedrich Nietzsche, the first philosopher to put his body on the line, warned against the way political events, the implacable rhetoric of politics, and recurring destructions would disturb your organs, making you want to puke. Shuttered by migraines and retching, Nietzsche dismantled any certitude we might have about separating work from life, thought from existence, and body from the pulse of malheur in political strife. Donning night goggles, Nietzsche also took it upon himself to capture futural flashes: in order to give a leg up to *philosophers of the future*, he had to calibrate the capacity for human figures of dominance to mutate and step away from false sovereignties. Ever becoming-woman, choosing Eve as the primal "gay scientist," Nietzsche made it a matter of duty to regender and multiply the existing possibilities of inhabiting different facets of *Geschlecht* (gender, genus), resetting the sexualities, adding question marks, implanting zoomorphic insets, sizing up difference among species, and breaking genus down. Nietzsche took time to review, in short, everything that would have sought to stabilize a concept of "humanity," suppressing its violent undertow and a history of severely mismanaged disavowal. Kant had already thrown in the towel regarding the *human as essence*, pointing out the instabilities of the human figure in its mutating self-production. It was not clear what the future would hold, as humanity lost substance and "man" no longer lined up as a refracted image of God. For his part, Kant had to pen in the wayward human through moral laws, short-leashing the autonomy of man. Becoming dangerous to itself, man as concept was on the ropes. Being and responsibility, caught in the ongoing destruction of *humanitas*, had to convene a summit meeting. The outer reaches of sovereignty appeared to muscle up mainly in acts of self-destruction. For what is more sovereign than running high on empty, itching to do away with oneself, and scaling back on exalted figures by means of willed extinction?

Intent on going down and stepping away, step by step, and by dint of purposeful overstep, Nietzsche practiced a takedown of European thought, aiming his star power at Hegel but also gunning for the startup troubleshooter, Kant. Only Spinoza, Goethe, Emerson, Brutus, and a few other breakout phenoms were kept on Team Nietzsche. The raids Nietzsche conducted were thoroughgoing, not sparing any piece of human or suprahuman substance, embodiment, or cultural strain. Nietzsche rooted out all sorts of stalwart claims while rummaging through the digestive tract. Sidelining the culinary and speculative habits associated with Germanity, Nietzsche not only scandalized contemporaries by turning French, but also began laying claim to an African spirit that pervaded the writing that came under the name "Friedrich Nietzsche" and the pseudonyms his work generated. For the transhuman shakeout that wanted more for us, beginning with a nonpessimistic practice of difference and *Dis-tanz*, Nietzsche taught us to *dance*, to take measure and calibrate the steps, to whirl without turning down or blindly denying the brunt of a nihilistic encroachment.

This work offers an analysis of America's turning mean and MAGA (Make America Great Again), tracking the incorporation of European racisms and seizing upon particular algorithms of social injustice, theoretically locked in. In a recent turn that has not ceased to run its course, something on the order of a nihilistic disclosure has been exposed in its distorted human carrier under the Germanic name "Trumpf." As alien, disturbing, and inassimilable as the invasiveness of the "Trump brand" has been since it crossed over from Germany to Queens to Manhattan, losing the "f" on the shuttle between Florida and Freiburg, it would be wrong to treat this alarming symptom only as a loathsome aberration – as if the Trumpfs had landed without secret roots in the makeup of an enlightened diction of commerce and mature social structures, supported by vigilant controls or philosophical setups. How fatiguing for us all!

Worn down, exhausted, dimmed, we increasingly feel that we can't go on, we must go on, leaning into the emptiness of an energy-sapping call. Concerning America's destinal downturn and the chronic misfiring of borrowed made-in-Germany nationalisms, it is by no means clear that traditional forms of argument and debate can be relied on to counter the hyperbolic stupidity consistent with an assemblage of handed-down cultural codes and their critical cohorts. We are in many ways backed against a hermeneutic wall, charged with filling in recalcitrant blanks, no matter how untimely this effort at understanding seems. It is not as if we did not know what has been happening it is rather that knowledge itself has fallen under a dictatorship of dunces traumatically mowing down the fields of any convincing recovery operation.

The depth of American anti-intellectualism – the astonishing *pride* of stupidity, politically pitched – must not be undermined. Nevertheless, we should keep alive the vibrancy of ambivalence and skeptical observation, putting ourselves on ambivalent alert. For it is the case that, at the same time as adopting dumbing and numbing attitudes of incomprehension, America, with nearly dialectical finesse, operates as an enormous reception center, a unique import–export hub, betting on a ground-level incapacity as the *only chance* for reoriginating stale inventories of European reasoning, be they incubated in ancient Greek thought or, frankly, made in America as a side hustle of university culture, still short on emergent world sectors of cultural ebullience.

Becoming woman, Nietzsche also became an early-bird hyphenated (French–, African–, Polish–, Swiss–, Italian–, Jewish–) American. The philosopher understood in prescient waves that thinking always abuts on a foreign exchange that is unavoidable, if barely calculable, according to his style of shredding identities and keeping the outside in, the foreign near. Heidegger tried to call Nietzsche home, like the straying boy in Lecture V of *What Is Called Thinking?* But she was gone. Set up, Nietzsche would not stick around for mystified nationalisms.

For us, the posture of standby ambivalence may be helpful when assessing these intercontinental problem sets. The theoretical overview that I propose may, in the case of unchecked

nationalisms, require the hypervigilance of con-
tinuing philosophical thought, some of which
has proven susceptible to relentless put-down
and anti-intellectual shaming in result-oriented
venues, to business-graded evaluation, and to
military overvaluation. The fine-grained practice of thought has been compromised not only
by public or medial downgrades but also by the
comorbidities that account for failures in the
philosophical household, no matter how strictly
supervised. In ways that have been mapped or
subjected to articulated directives, philosophy
tends to chase down the mirage of public space,
yet mostly finds itself trembling in a toss-up
between home and abroad, riding unamendable
effects of expulsion: house-hunting and homebound, the philosophical instinct also puts one on
the run, whether one seeks a hideout or is coerced
into exilic retreat, at once fearing and fetishizing
the foreign. The spin of double duty (running
off *and* homebound, fearing *and* fetishizing)
should not surprise us if we lean on poetry for
strength of purpose, acknowledging the poetic
penchant for witnessing on behalf of philosophical thought. *One can only appropriate
what is foreign, says Hölderlin*. At this

point I want to hitch a ride on something that presses us still today: a phrasing that Philippe Lacoue-Labarthe has offered in *Heidegger and the Politics of Poetry*. When evoking themes of an implicit turf war between poetry and philosophy, he makes it a matter of "taking measure of an epoch (with which we are far from finished) and of the philosophical questioning that subtends it: Our politics, and not only our politics, still depend on it."[1] Every mythologeme embedded in nationhood, its sovereign inflation and inevitable collapse, attaches back to a philosophical appropriation of poetry, no matter how deeply concealed in the playoffs of degraded language games.

*****

We cannot be sure that the identity tags placed on philosophical thought are valid anymore. Still desired but to a large degree outsmarted by crushing blights and trending materialities, philosophy has been consistently called out, limping off the world stage. Nonetheless, its falling stature and felt perishability may offer us an inroad, even as its predicament drives a hard bargain. *Philosophy is never where you expect to find it.* Scaled for obsolescence, prone to the displacement of value, caught short by aberrant tropologies, it is bloated with fade-outs and congested rhetorical byways, routinely mismanaged by conceptual handlers of all stripes – or simply *too smart for its own good* in our age of straight-shooting calibration and moralistic overdrive. It carries a legacy of broken promises and flubbed transcendence. Still, the philosophical attitude compels respect, a kind of Achtung delivered by Kant, "the Moses of our nation," according to Hölderlin. Kant was a lawgiver who pondered the peculiar *popularity* of philosophical investigation – an enduring enigma, be it in the common language sought by Wittgenstein or in concert with the being-in-common of Jean-Luc Nancy. Even as it appears to take a series of curtain calls or to trade up for the privilege of formal logic, philosophy shows a pulse, answers to the vibrancy of an existential need in terms spelled out by Husserl, who signaled the *need* for philosophy in our lives. How does this work?

Snubbing the presumption of relevance and bypassing clamors for identifiable forms of life-emboldening encouragement, philosophical assertion often misses the mark as it makes its mark. As Derrida said of Lacoue-Labarthe's work, it *desists*, tensed somewhere between resistance and retreat, where it lies in wait, possibly for a long while, subsisting on its own poverty.

Supplied by Hölderlin with motifs of *Dürftigkeit* (wretchedness) and *Armut* (indigence) – the experience of depleted Being – and superintended by Wittgenstein and Heidegger according to different protocols, philosophy has taken long stretches of downtime, as if it were meant to lay fallow or play dead, stupefied by the shortfall of its limits. The way it embarrasses itself, stirs, or self-deflates is what interests us here, as it is drawn to probing scenes of violence and retreat, to measuring the incapacitation of language when it comes to making good on its promissory peace treaty. In some districts of Saying, it binds a destiny where no one seriously advocates the destinal quality of philosophical directives, peculiar coaching techniques, and bleary-eyed discovery. Still, there is something about its way of emptying out or grinding to a halt that has become increasingly compelling. *Philosophy is never where you expect to find it* – a contention made by Nancy that succeeds in opening up entire continents of thought, where unpredictable considerations come into play and once reliable programs are fatefully deactivated.

Making sense of America requires another relation to sense, a different approach to meaning and its appointed objects. For Nancy, the destruction of meaning is itself part of our engagement with meaning. The question of finding, losing, or relocating meaning has a long history in philosophy, leaving a record of stray shots and deviations from marked paths, the *methodos* (mode of investigation) on which philosophy depends without being able to pinpoint a viable route, or routine, that would provide sense and direction (*du sens*).

Perhaps Nancy was himself vibing off a critical contention made by Derrida about an aspect of psychoanalysis. In *The Post Card*, when taking on Lacan's reading of "The Purloined Letter," Derrida notes that Lacan retrieves the phallus where he expected to find it – between the cheeks of the chimney. The keyed-up signifier is always where psychoanalysts *expect* to find the prize, unintercepted, locked into place. The predictability of a letter's trajectory is part of the old quarrel over whether a letter reaches its destination or is constitutively fated to miss its mark, drop into a dead letter box, deviate or abort a planned arrival, perverting the course of *l'être-lettre* (the being-letter), a *Geschick* (destiny) of *Schicksal* (fate) and related send-offs. With no deterrent or seductive corrosiveness blocking its way, the signifier is nonetheless given to stalls, upending an itinerary en route, no matter how securely plotted. Poe's text, itself an allegory of displacement and dazzled stagnation, priming the incessant threat of political payback, tracks a letter's improbable retrieval, bringing us to a zone where plots attached to "America" and "Europe" emerge to exchange blows in a territorial dispute over letters and Being, their addressability and burn points.

With its renewable travel pass to areas of thought and Being, both remote and familiar, prone to "destinerring" or clinched to a still-stand of extreme passivity, philosophy establishes boundaries that would require the services of Kafka's land surveyor, who measures the expanse of a language-dependent region of thought on the basis of precariously shifting grounds, and whose legitimate limits are barely ascertainable. Wittgenstein and others – on both sides of the Atlantic – wondered whether America had anything to contribute to philosophy. Or was it rather some impoverished outland where thought goes to die? Can poetry seriously flourish in such a vacant lot, reserved for Being's steady destitution and wordless drop-off site? It has seemed to a number of grand commentators, moreover, that the jointure of philosophy and politics has been doomed to buckle under the pressure of such nullity. Maybe so – at least according to a specific algorithm of usefulness and the language centers that still prime philosophical thought, chasing off the serious dives of poetic utterance.

– There's an outside chance, though, that the near *vacancy* of inheritable tropologies offers an opportunity for a different kind of representation and critical inflection, grounded in the exigencies of a more hardened experience of poverty. At the juncture of sober calibration and combative discord, one agreement has been passed: the distress of philosophical reflection, when its loss of ground is not in dispute, comes to be showcased by and in "America," which continues to supply a huge depot for foreign discursivities. Interestingly, the *foreign* is also situated at the heart of the American adventure, self-alienating and broken, affined to the etymological setup of "Brooklyn": a "broken land" (Dutch *breuckelen*), foreign to itself and speaking the common language in a dialect. One must ask whether any nation state fronted by the performative ploy of "united" is not masking disintegration and the spread of noxious break-off points. Let me refocus, then, the largely uninterrogated philosopheme "America," the United States of said historical entity, in order to score a philosophical point.

Chronically exposed to habits of destruction turned inward (though any purported inside assures outward symptoms, spreading and contaminating a worlding world), "America" enjoins us to revisit its philosophical properties – to examine how, since the nineteenth century, it has compelled puzzled commentary and provoked competitive strife with its European counterparts. In the *Communist Manifesto* Marx and Engels look to a version of America that comes close to gaining their approval. They mark the young nation up for inventing an unheard-of vitality and the historically vibrant verve of voracity, endorsing an exemplary, if violent, growth plan. "America" hosts all sorts of aporetic appraisals to which European philosophy resorts when ducking self-appraisal or (for the most part) when building on a handily circumscribed deficit of thought. All in all, "America" is hard to fix, but pulsates a residue of meaning where the gods have not quite fled, but never bothered to tour – a retreat of source and ground of which it was never a claimant in the first place. Squatting in conceptual hideouts, this imposing strip of land meaning and contradictory impulse has also sucked vital energies, reinvented outposts of greed, yet succored *dreams*, promoted getaways, and housed the fabled outcasts of its plurimutational heritage.

Whether an aggregate of nations lets its subjects dream may look like a secondary tropological concern for the discipline of political science. Freud, whose analyses explicated and expanded the field, delivered political heft when analyzing the covert operations of malcontents and parricidal influencers, social infrastructures and the slips of aggressive coexistence. He shared with Plato a sense for how polis and nation builders manage the anarchic unconscious, regardless of whether it goes collective or stays singular. The way a citizenry dreams and crawls into nighttime – lifting repression, indulging taboos, allowing for the expulsion of the superego and altering the promise of light-filled representation – is something that specifically concerned Plato as he was considering the lures of the *tyrannical soul structure* in governance. It took him nine books to overturn the hypothesis that tyrants have more fun. One can be released to one's own tyrannical recognizance after dusk falls, when turning in. At night, every citizen gets a free pass to disinhibition by means of bubbling incest, murder, and related morphs of violent trespass, sidelining state restrictions with deregulated license, allowing for represented actions that contrast with terms set for a diurnal polis – a serious problem for political watchdogs, since it is never sure whether the dreaming demos can clear out its transgressive romps by daylight and return to the realm of the laws.

The continued presumptions of the "American dream" – including the desperate poetry of homegrown dreamers, an increasingly marginalized population of native immigrants – call up another logic of governance and repressive disturbances. An important aspect of a dream logic injected into the political sphere involves impulses of criminal abandon and motifs of ungrounding and disorientation – crucial categories that Stanley Cavell, philosophizing America via Emerson and Wittgenstein, draws up in corollary terms of *founding*, *foundering*, and *foundling*. For "America," ever on the hunt for founding mythemes, consistently founders, skidding on calculated reversions to the founding fathers of a foundling nation. "America" takes hits from foreign philosophers of the last centuries, but also goes after parts of itself, destroying its own capacity for adding to or cutting away fruitfully from the premises of European inheritability, to which it owes a credible, if false-positive, sense of history and ambivalent co-belonging. In some ways, America gives up too quickly on dreaming, ruthlessly supplanting the returns of fantasy with the capital real, a run-up surrogate for the American dream, and racist subventions.

*****

The viral shock detonated by an accelerated rhythm of conquest to which, according to Mary Shelley, the Americas were from the start exposed by the Europeans, gives us an inkling of what could have become of the territories – and in particular the colonies – if only America had been discovered more *gradually*, without the ruthless offence signaled at the starting gate of fast-paced violent incursion. The original bursts of genocidal attack and land theft would leave an inerasable stain, sometimes waiting out down-the-line syndromic outbursts, in latency. Mary Shelley does not rule out conquest, but puts it on a different timer. Philosophically, the ambivalence ascribed to the sudden overturning of values, identities, and forms of pre-technological prowess – in addition to other fast-tracking and questionable morphs of "manifest destiny" – overruns the conception of nationhood as an onto-theological home base.

For the big guns of poesy and thought, what they called "America" readily became the headquarters for *Entgötterung* (de-divinization, Heidegger) or *Entzauberung* (disenchantment, Max Weber): the accelerant to an absenting of the divine on which the new continent seemed monstrously set, exposing the world to an experience of loss and foundering so radical that it stunted philosophical growth or coherent claims of sovereignty. If it had been caught in time, America's founding–foundering could have been poetically decried, according to Shelley's theory, or perhaps even *understood* in terms of its potentiating range and ongoing implications, a prequel to the Trail of Tears. Nor did everyone require of America originary myths or serious saga – the Saying that opens to the sacred on which Heidegger relies for instituting a top-tier version of elected nationhood, a far-reaching, if destructive, political fantasy. America, for its part, is left in the speculative dust, with smatters and slogans such as "In God we trust" obsessively repeated in juridical precincts, yet resolutely ambiguous as grounding language in the epoch after God's death. How seriously, in the end, can a conceded form of blindness be taken – "blind trust" as syntagm for acts of trust – given the flimsy performative sanctions of trusting, part of a signifying device that removes trust from truth? Neither beholden to truth nor guarantor of knowledge, trust implicates and builds off mistrust – a primary hermeneutic condition. What kind of temper and temporality does "trust in God" presuppose or establish? One would have to study the rhetorical breakaway of trust from faith at this point, when parsing the "we" that pivots around in the trusting assertion "In God *we* trust." Emerson purposefully switches to self-confidence, *trust in self*, when seeking to found a specifically American philosophy.

Ambivalence comes to America from all sides, from inside out, along neurotically secured borders, in common language troves, from global reaches beyond settled borders. As a category that has not ceased to arouse political energy, annulling and generating worlds at the same time, the "new world" invites different levels of reflection on European thought, its emissaries, return cycles, and the steady leakages or distortions for which "America" has been held responsible. Object of fascination and dread, evaluated at once as generative ebullience and bubbling pollutant, short on authority but high on obstinate fictions of autonomy, enchanted by its own hype of goodness, "America" has forced European thought to read itself reading, rejecting, separating off, and making speculative allowances for staying back in more or less secured philosophical precincts and sanctuarized areas of poetic dare.

The skeptical tour of "America" that we find announced in key European texts does not prevent the European poet from thematizing and thinking, with near-obsessive clarity, the ontological pressures of despiritualized existence, a wind tunnel of unshieldedness, designating unprotected acts of poetic utterance and extreme exposures – what Hölderlin and Benjamin see as the essential job description of the poetic vocation, pitched as alone-standing witness. Concerning what it takes to affirm this vocation – the courage, and even the *rage* in *courage* minted in modernity by Lessing through the unleashing of his specific brand of *anger* – we would want to see how poeticity stifles or reroutes historical anger, finds it another home, where the lots are vacant and the gods have shunned, conceding our earthbound predicament as houseless, deserted, and famished. I will not succumb to further generalizations or the fly-by phrasing of quasi-transcendence. Let me just say at this point that Lessing's poetic anger is of political consequence, leading the immigrant Hannah Arendt to take up a theory of *justified anger*, others to pursue the theme of *indignity*, still others to pull up a history of *angry women*, and still others to monitor attacks issued from the vitriolic supremacist, who hangs a coded portrait of the "angry Black man." Nor should we remain insensitive to the maimed trans body in Hedwig's "angry inch." How many types of anger, undertheorized, feed the political agony of the day?

Although often doomed as the short fuse of action, reactive and frustrated, anger refers us in the end to law and justice: it implies a theory of rights. Framed in deficiency of aim and failing any measure of just return, anger lines up, since Lessing's reprisal of classically straitened rage, on the side of reason. Thus, a few years ago, one of my Slovenian friends, I believe it was Alenka Zupančič, supplied and parsed the utterance, apropos of Friedrich Schiller, "I have reason to be angry."[2] To the extent that anger's home base has recourse to reason and law, it also presupposes speech. Even when flustered, anger demands language, wanting its day in court; we see it from the robber in Schiller to the population of post-punk destitutes and to the *misérables* of global injustice. In the punk-pulsated Hedwig drama, the "angry inch" of German castration was expressly commissioned by an occupying American military officer. Hedwig, a trans philosopher, had been expelled from the university because of a thesis that analyzed the influence of aggressive German philosophy on the genesis of rock and roll. The East German protagonist, a student so poor that, as a child, they "lived in an oven" in mother's tiny apartment, received a massive dose of inculcation – a surviving inkling of *Bildung* (education) – from the blaring radio broadcast of rock: a sliver of early Rammstein, namely the Neue Deutsche Härte band, which fused American cultural and military bases with German rehabilitation and education. The political shards, drugs, and poverty that link the two cultures in a mutually repressive hold still need to be told. Even Elvis went to Germany, having been instructed to "do nothing to embarrass your country,"[3] and Jim Morrison doted on Nietzsche. As for the *Angry Inch* of Hedwig the German scholar, it veers toward an obsession with Jews: the film is suffused with images of Jewish spectators as it flashes Hebrew lettering, part of an inerasable haunting that attends any memory henceforth, no matter how receded or tattered, crazed or ghost-dunked, of historical recounting in overlapping Germano-American fields.

*****

For contenders on the American side of a reflective debate, it was no longer clear, following earnest questioning, whether European philosophy, after Hegel's completion of philosophy, was at all inheritable – or in any way a viably exportable object, retrofitted to the rest of the world. But even the stark limits imposed by the hypothesis of finite inheritability and the inherent restrictions of relay, decoding mechanisms, appropriation, transfer, and partial historical recall require a responsible understanding of where we stand, a determination of how differences are dealt. As in the Kafkan text, American pickup games can subsist on a mote, pounce on crumbs, and ride their impoverishment while claiming grandeur and boasting a knack for supersized recklessness. [§Sidebar] Much of the resentment against Derrida involves his translocations, the way his travel itinerary instigated a kind of re-origination of thought, developed in part on troubled American grounds. The allegorical adjustment he advocated was in some manner disparaged by hard-core European philosophers and repackaged by American receptors. [StopSidebar]

As rebel, as child, the United States did not need "old Europe," a split off part of itself, to pollute and question its premises; we were doing it to ourselves, shooting ourselves in the legacies, undermining ideals set up only to be shot down. In Emerson's famous essay "Self-Reliance," a history of ambivalence turns into *aversion*, which means, for him, the aversion of conformity. Self-reliance sounds the call for a level of permanent pushback that does not cut off decisively from past affiliation, and from which one must beat a consistent retreat while holding onto and inventing its fringes. Emerson's thought of self-reliance in aversion prompts Stanley Cavell's breakdowns: "[I]t means that this writing finds America, as it stands, or presents itself, to be repellent, or say unattractive; and it means that America so finds this writing. Emerson by no means, however, just shrinks from America, because this 'aversion' turns not just away, but at the same time, and always, toward America."[4] The aversive swerve is "an Emersonian calculation of the unapproachable, a reckoning of it as the forbidding. What about America is forbidding, prohibitive, negative," compelling a return to a reprehensive topic or topology that horrifies and attracts the rookie philosophy?

What Emerson wishes to show is, in Cavell's words, that, "for all our empiricism, nothing (now) makes an impression on us, that we accordingly have no experience (of our own), that we are inexperienced. Hence Emerson's writing is meant as the provision of experience for these shores, of our trials, perils, essays."[5] In this text as well as in "The American Scholar," Emerson aims to reconstitute the founding of a nation, "acts of founding and findings, findings of losses and lost ways, this falling and befalling, images of, or imaged by, the loss of a child . . . the idea of the child as founder . . . showing that its writer has found nothing." There is a Nietzschean itinerary shaping the way the New World philosophy warms up, prepping an initiatory leap: as in Zarathustra's proclamation, one must lose the sage before finding her. The inapproachable sets up Heidegger's attempted rescue of Nietzsche as well, exhorting us to lose the work before presuming to find it. "In a new world, everything is to be lost and everything is to be found."[6]

Looking for America – much like looking for Nietzsche in Heidegger's *Was heißt denken?* – means knowing how to forget or lose it, how to affirm or deal with an already lost ground of the risked experiment. In this regard (to step on the accelerator), the search itself draws a contract with Nietzsche's *Gay Science* and related texts that count on blowing up their premises by trial, essay, peril, retraction, repulsion, and return, on finding the bug or hypocritical practice, and on gearing up from the start line of inexperience. Emerson, for his part, calculates the returns of America, the acts of writing and self-reliance that betray from the start an internal competition of faltering sovereignty and the thrill kill for which these acts are henceforth pumped. At one point America was young, untried, yet to be proven. It was writing its own ticket, high on self-endangerment and frontier mythology. These skids provide the categoremes on which Nietzsche's text has hitched a ride and America has stashed its dose of insubstantiality. The only difference here is that Cavell bets on the returns, offering symmetry and the expectation that "everything can be found" after radical loss and nationalist potlatch . . .

*****

When Heidegger famously said, in a 1966 interview, *Nur noch ein Gott kann uns retten*, "Only a god can save us," he was ruling out America, which he, together with the high priests of poetry and thought, considered to be godless, a voided space of portentous consequence, technologically humming while spiritually stalled. The sentence, issued posthumously – Lacoue-Labarthe calls it a "testamentary" sentence – refers to an *uns* ("us") that remains admittedly ambiguous after all the draining that Heidegger accomplished on the subject of history, driving the western figure and self-overcoming of "man." The status of *uns* in his statement is not definitively settled. For the most part, Heidegger's rhetoric of assemblage evinces a gathering of beings and the volk, as Levinas observed, that leads to a portentous flex of *uns*, "us" – or, shifting ground, disfigures the "we" in any performative application of *We, the People*. (What is more, one could say, together with Nancy, that "in" from "being-in-the-world" is not assured either: where is this "in" of world, especially when the "world" has been upended?) In statements made by Heidegger and others, the referential authority of "America" does not seem to be in question, however, but indicates a condemned site whose epicenter, the United States, circumscribes the outer limits of western metaphysics – posthumously settled, leaking fumes, and broken by the unhindered sway of technology. There is nothing rescuable about the American menace that Heidegger and others disparage, only rarely pausing their phobic appropriations of a land reshaped by European rejects. Still, Heidegger called upon us to think through to the depth of what we condemn. In many ways, thinking and its philosophical allies have held up "America" as an inhospitable site of spiritual recalcitrance linked to technological blindness, a reckoning of the ruthless drivenness by which the American dream is fueled, providing at best only a limit case of temporal initiative in terms of what can be inherited, integrated, and retained – or even safely disposed of, trashed.

*****

Let us re-approach the unapproachable. Often disavowed or introjected – psychically horded as an obsolesced part object – Greek tragedy sets up and recycles the parameters of political action and heroic mythemes. Some of the fight zones established by the dilemma typical of Greek tragedy involve a single figure that defies a sacred decree and other law-generating instances. Aspects of ancient trespass continue to develop and devolve, streamlined to sordid campaign aesthetics, pitting a solitary rogue contender against a community where law abiders clash with lawbreakers, in a Benjaminian contest of rival forces and crash zones.

In American scenes of recycled tragic postures, ground down to various morphs of contestatory depravity, the criminal mug profiles heroic attributes. We can look to the measure, considered by Hegel or reinscribed by Hölderlin, of what holds up as holy or unholy in Greek tragedy, where the battle of new gods against old gods is still being fought. These kinds of struggles, though bared of transcendence, cast light on a haunting by religion, part of the unfolding of western metaphysics, analyzed by Lacoue-Labarthe as the possibility or opening of the sacred, in view of the "stubborn denial of all religiosity (the *religio* is a Roman concept)."[7] What interests me in these reflections is not only the grave reversion to the wars of the gods (still popular as Titans, supernatural gangs, and emergent colliding worlds) – wars that come up in different genres of American representations, releasing signs of inscription and fascination in so many reunions of cartoonish Übermenschen that have migrated to American scenes of writing and projection – but the way our shared worlds hold the traces of these battles, which continue to undergird conflicts and our valued fight spirit, no matter how displaced, sublimated, partially voided, or transvaluated into various nationalist arenas of contest they are. The consistent rebranding of the gods and of the opposing insinuations of ungodliness reveals a logic of residual transcendence that scatters the sacred elsewhere. Still on demand, the value of *sacrifice* becomes nonetheless meaningless when war no longer functions as a pregnancy test for historical becoming, as it did in Hegel, pushing through to the horizon of new world meaning, to a resignifying of order, even though the vocabulary of sacred contestation persists. Where we no longer know how to wage war as part of *Sinnbildung* (meaning creation), of a project of making sense – such as claims that war unblocks history and brings or defends democracy, framing egregious behaviors – that bears momentous reckonings, we fall into another existential category, another kind of voided space over which "America" in some ways prevails. New yet tethered, unable to break loose from a past that won't pass, we are prone, in this slice of epochality, to repeat and relay destructive runs of ancient representations, emptied of authority, released from sacred propulsion and thin on justificatory discourses. As Nietzsche surmised, this faltering *Sinnbildung* is something that "America" knows about itself, sometimes turning this knowledge to advantage.

*****

If "America" is doomed to be ruled out of an alliance of philosophical validity imagined by philosophers and poets, including the homegrown crop, this also means that it raises a problem, it is a contender, which has implications especially for Europe and for the worlds to which we hold, in distress – these fissured refractions of philosophical nations that underlie decision-making and the legitimacy of self-questioning. Heidegger writes in one of his lectures of 1936: "Even the doom of the absence of the god is a way in which the world worlds."[8]

Let me world now to the designated alias of the United States, "America," as philosophical nemesis.

Stanley Cavell's discovery of America, guided by the texts of Emerson and Thoreau, deals head-on with an "experience and disappointment directed to one's culture as a whole (hence to oneself as compromised in the culture)." Sounding Emerson's "Self-Reliance" as an aversion to conformity, he names a "comparable spiritual territory" in Wittgenstein's *Investigations* that evinces an "explicit disgust." Cavell focuses on the famous description in the Preface to the *Investigations*, a text that bears "this work, in its poverty and in the darkness of its time," and shows its empty hand, "its apparent denials; its embarrassments. . . . and madness." The impoverishing condition on which and from which he works holds that "poverty is not a simple expression of humility but a stern message: the therapy prescribed to bring light into the darkness of the time that will present itself as, will itself be, starvation; as if our philosophical spirit is indulged, farced to the point of death."[9] Wittgenstein's radical insistence that starvation be prescribed to his readers indicates the brunt of an inescapable imperative. Undergirding philosophical exertion, Wittgenstein "is fully clear" in revealing "his awareness that readers will (should) feel deprived by his teaching."[10] Cavell calls the philosophical tightening a therapy, seeing the fulfillment of its task as a light-bearing therapy.

"Poverty as a condition of philosophy," writes Cavell, "is hardly a new idea." Emerson "deploys it as an idea specifically of America's deprivations, its bleakness and distance from Europe's achievements, as constituting America's necessity, and its opportunity, for finding itself."[11] Separating off from an overladen charge of European tradition, America paradoxically crawls in the dust to assert something like an original authority, at times lacking the will or the need to propose even a pretend basis for the legitimacy of a restart. There is something of a Kantian gesture in this hunger crawl, because, in a nearly dialectical swerve, poverty becomes its fortune, as Kant's inability to write like Moses (Mendelssohn) becomes henceforth a virtue – and a model – for the overriding power of cloddy philosophical writing. Cavell's commentary: "I read: The poverty that, morally speaking, is pleasing to the God and affords us access to the humanity of others – it is its poverty, not its riches, that constitutes America's claim upon others – is, philosophically speaking, our access to necessity, our route out of privacy."[12] These vital claims on impoverishing authority are parenthetically stated in a note on the end of "Experience," which hides out in a textual mine.

Cavell continues, breaking ground for the unaccommodated. The impoverished reader whom the European tradition disdains becomes a vehicle for negotiating a peace treaty with the inheritable aspects of philosophical mainstays: "Others take Emerson to advise America to ignore Europe; to me his practice means that part of the task of discovering philosophy in America is discovering terms in which it is given to us to inherit the philosophy of Europe. Its legacy may hardly look like philosophy at all, but perhaps rather like an odd development in literature. By European patterns, Americans will seem, in Thoreau's phrase, '*poor* students,' the phrase by which Thoreau identifies the unaccommodated who are his rightful readers."[13] The brunt of poverty, a barely recognizable feature of the tradition that is sidelined to margins of disavowal, travels among different conceptual *milieux* on which, in American writing, literary and philosophical usages of language depend. American *theory* (an undecidable limit between literature and philosophy) henceforth covers a friable ground ranging from miserable material conditions to the limited resources of the struggling student, the "rightful" reader on Thoreau's roster.

Poverty binds the clashing cultures, soothing an Oedipal rage. Poverty, as revolutionary wounding, becomes as important to originating an American relation to reference and thought as it was to Wordsworth or Rousseau – and to Victor Hugo, if we are to call up the great European novels of the nineteenth century whose destitute characters sorely scraped by on a ground level of subsistence. In a way poverty, keeping everyone down, unleashes a democratic strain of viral proportions, pre-globally cast, felling or potentially wrangling each and all to the ground, flashing in the discordant worlds a constant threat of a mobile "creditory"–predatory clampdown. The specter of poverty, its encroaching strike or stubborn facticity, affects those outside the genocidal firing range, instigating another kind of murder spree that obsesses American letters and a referential debt to the material sprawl. The rough conditions of an impoverished order of being, gaining the upper hand in American letters, reroute thinking and some of the critical presumptions on which it may have relied. Poetically and philosophically recognized, the motif of poverty, as it spreads, maintains an edge as thematic crumb and material dredge to the degree that it makes *everything* appropriable, including the dusty shimmer of pretend knowledge and the increasingly jacked hankering of ruthless acquisition.

*

Beyond the theoretical pertinence and empirical solidity of Cavell's inquiry, the reflections he offers on America repeatedly indicate a nonthematizable encroachment under whose sway he watchfully proceeds. He is not the only philosopher to be swarmed by a ghostly entourage as he seeks to encounter the mutinous depth of his object. He is clear about the otherworldly facets of this study, at least clear enough to allude strongly to an *effect of the phantom* that underlies the investigation he conducts on the *Investigations*, loitering in the vicinity of Heidegger and Emerson in addition to – or by virtue of – a spectral cohort that invades his own thought. When reckoning with American impoverishment in philosophical slums or neighborhoods, and doing it in terms of historical allowance, Cavell avers a double haunting, as he attunes to Wittgenstein's air. When reading the heir, questioning the knots and nots of inheritability, he sheds light on a

Shakespearean convocation that calls together the nexus of *heirs*, *airs*, and *heirlooms*.

[*§Sidebar*] *You may think that I am merely brushing up against an unhinged signifier, or putting on airs.* Not at all. The rapport between speculation and "spookulation" has been a longtime pursuit for me, urged by Shakespeare and Cervantes, pinpointed by Kant, prompted by Goethe, goaded by Hegel, interiorized by Nietzsche, poked by Swedenborg and Schnitzler, followed up by Freud, spectrally recast by Derrida, thwarted by Acker, seized by Lispector, and dignified in Cixous, among premier ghost catchers and those in convo with Marx. [*StopSidebar*] Cavell cops to the haunted disposition to which the study owes its subtle uprisings without going so far as to risk losing his bearings, though losing bearings and bungling earthly markers is part of his challenge to self. When writing the text on America, he is plainly haunted, as he *repeats*, finding and losing himself off course. By dint of a spooked venture consciously offered, the critical reader, no matter how impoverished, is far less constrained than in other contexts to dig up latent signifiers plotted in invisible ink and Wolfman-like magic words, or – when anxiously made to follow underground logic and cover-up rhetoric – ploys that double in more unconscious regions for a pretend solidity of means and method. There is yet another bow he makes to a phantom procession spiriting and carrying through his probe, creating a double framing that I'd like to acknowledge before proceeding.

The other configuration impels the text toward allegorization. Urged on by a compulsion, Cavell seeks the cause of ungroundedness that hacks into "America," revealing a chip that obsesses, haunts the writer, taunts the heritage he thought to have understood, inflects a shaky reception reluctantly welcomed, if in a mode of *aversion*. According to Cavell's frank confession, the first haunting from which the text on America emerges involves a stunned discovery made by the philosopher, one that pushes him away from the relative safety of Richard Rorty and the often rhetorical squabble with pragmatists or the trail of transcendentalists. Veering away from the course charted by his academic writing career, he suddenly comes upon two sets of European thought mines. Stunned and staggered, Cavell encounters for the first time texts signed by Nancy and Lacoue-Labarthe, as well as, in a subsequent sitting or séance, the theories of the phantom proposed by Nicolas Abraham and Maria Torok, commented upon by Derrida who, when analyzing the post-Freudian theory of the phantom, stalks and stakes condemned sites in the preface to their work.[14]

Both teams (Lacoue-Labarthe–Nancy; Derrida–Abraham–Torok) feature at the starting gate of Carvell's *This New yet Unapproachable America* as apparitions that startle the American philosopher, who finds his worlds sideswiped and reconfigured, severely questioned and refreshed. A new Euro-American alliance is called up, in a maneuver that determines the irremediable breaking points of American thought. I shall start with the second instance of haunted avowal, where a traumatic encounter prods Cavell to reappropriate his own work and that of his usual suspects, no longer recognizable to him simply as Mssrs. Emerson and Thoreau, yet more compelling– cavelling in the shattered urgency of their spectral appeal and the delivery systems of European rerouting.

*****

Stupefied and haunted, he is on the way to the language of Hölderlin's elegy "Bread and Wine." Swerving to German poetry, Cavell repeats the question, "*wozu Dichter in dürftiger Zeit?*" ("why poets in a time of need?"). Why do we need poets in times of radical deprivation, clutching to those squeezed by "starvation"? How is it that we rely on the poetic word in the time of depleted figures, when stranded with the broken pump of promising and positing, clenched by material drought and spiritual emptying? How does philosophy stay popular, even unread and half dead, while poetry, skinned and shivering, keeps guard over scarcity, its own and that of others and defeated worlds – overseeing the "unaccommodated" have-nots, the "*poor* student" of Thoreau's predilection, his elected addressee? How does the imago of Kafka's inerasable "Hunger Artist" come to preside with vigorous dignity over these scenes of spent nurturance? Impoverishment presents a prime calling card of philosophical modes of destitution to which Socrates' fashion sense already attested. The scandal of impoverishment, its stripped-down exposition and persecuted forbearance, cuts an intolerable figure of widespread wretchedness to some, yet remains a staple of the Christian calling and poetic sound-outs, the Walpurgisnacht of beggars, a preview of Hölderlin's elegiac haunt.

*****

Scouring the ravine of philosophical output, Wittgenstein appears to scrape against a barren heritage, bottoming out on "an impoverished idea of philosophy in its own systematic shunning, its radical discounting, or recounting, of philosophical terms and arguments and results, its relentless project to, perhaps we can say, desublimize thought."[15] It is here that Cavell picks up the theme of his own haunting, if almost inadvertently, as a subtle recurrence in the space of his strapped investigation. "So I am understandably haunted by a reaction Wittgenstein in 1931 is reported by [Friedrich] Waismann to have expressed concerning [Moritz] Schlick's teaching in an American university: 'What can we give the Americans? Our half-decayed culture? The Americans have as yet no culture. But from us they have nothing to learn. . . . Our talk hasn't

the force to move anything.'"[16] Cavell argues
that, in questioning "whether Europe's central
thought is inheritable further West and further East Wittgenstein is expressing an anxiety
over whether Europe itself will go on inheriting
philosophy; whether he, who represents a present philosophy, can hand on his thoughts to
another generation. If philosophy is to continue
it must continue to be inherited." With Cavell
signaling to *Wozu Dichter*, we note that philosophy in crisis often turns to poetic utterance as a
bailout, keeping close to an ambivalently held
address, desperately sought. Let us continue. The
principal concern of philosophy henceforth is
organized not so much around its originality, as
Cavell points out, "but over its intelligibility to
another generation – call this its historical power
to go on – apart from which the path may be
lost."[17] A lot is going on in these key passages,
each strand of which deserves its own dossier and
careful consideration.

One of the instigating concerns mentioned
by Cavell, perhaps not as urgently imposing
as the consequence of historicity and the reliance on intelligibility that organize his thought
on America, involves the common disbursal of

transfer tickets to universities – the way brainy Europeans fly over to America to teach, without awakening in the American professoriate the expectation of a reciprocal booking. It would be wrong lightly to insist that Europeans practice a slammed door policy, even though the exchanges are indisputably lopsided, non-equivalent in terms of conferral of cultural value and general approbation of the learned laureate. Wittgenstein questions the very premises of an exercise that ships European professors to American institutions, a habit that operates on the uninterrogated assumption that the Europeans have something to teach. The full implications of these transfers and the bartered volleys of transatlantic translation would benefit, no doubt, from a survey that consisted of pedagogical destination, layovers, the handling of visas, class enrollment figures, remuneration, and other technologies of sponsorship, in addition to a speculative analysis of the imaginary profit margins of foreign exchange as part of higher education. In the meanwhile, American institutions are reducing language requirements and down-dosing on reading practices.

*****

Working up the conditions of "worlding" and its American counterparts, Cavell was concerned with philosophical accounting and how things could move ahead. The study begins to transvaluate a motif that threatens irreversible slowdown and previews philosophical attrition – that of penury, that is, of the diminishment of means and historical commission. Cavell flips these terms into viable attributes, holding up an inverted American trophy: the *prestige of atrophy*, premature and lasting, positing an originary markdown. The Europeans begin to plead decadence and fear of obsolescence. Reserved for the other side of the Atlantic, as provisional counterweight, is the conjectured matter of "naïveté," the fable of stunted growth: cowing to this hypothesis, refreshing it with a strike of transvaluation, we could say that there is something about American immaturity that, in one corner, kicks off another kind of cultural competition and scientific–mathematical–musical compulsion, an institutional Disneyland, spelling out the advances of kids' stuff.

Cavell also makes an altogether different point, meant to assure an historical transfer of thought when classifying the philosophical files whose very inheritability remains in question. Sizing the hurdles, he relies on *intelligibility* as a principle of generational outreach and sustainability, a point of philosophy's resilience and time climb. There are moments when he pulls out of a hermeneutic gridlock in order to accelerate the cause of philosophy, supplied as it is at one bend with the lure of intelligibility, its capacity for transfer and conceptual repurposing. In order to strengthen a viable edge of intelligibility, Cavell must remove blockages that his argument also indicates. How is the petition for intelligibility compromised (or bolstered) by the ungrounded persistence of that which exceeds reason and understanding? The work at hand, he argues, is haunted or inspirited. It is dragged along by an otherworldly spirit, inspirited – inspired – by the work of Nancy and Lacoue-Labarthe on the German romantics, one of whose lead singers is Friedrich Schlegel. Reinventing the fragment as a stand-alone break-off point (without an implied totality), Schlegel, together with his brother, called for the suturing of philosophy and poetry, revealing the seriousness of literature for thought in terms of "the literary absolute" (the title of Lacoue-Labarthe and Nancy's study). Friedrich also wrote the important essay "Über die Unverständlichkeit" ("On Incomprehensibility"), which, to the degree that a title means what it says, puts a premium on *unintelligibility* by highlighting the incompletion of sense-making on which claims of inheritability subsist. On the basis of this groundbreaking work, one can argue, in amicable riposte to Cavell, that intelligibility – a presumption that might not survive basic testability standards – would be *the kiss of death* to transfer mechanisms and claims of futurity in thought. At the very least, an uninterrogated standard of intelligibility would close the book on serious study, which, after the Schlegel bros, should place bets on a daring grapple with the *unintelligible* relay of materials and acts of signification, riding the residue of an inexhaustible text. Well, certainly the "poor" American student, "unaccommodated," will not find the European teacher to hold pace with the assumption of intelligibility and its looming counterpart – a topos and value that invites more critical reflection, given that literature put out a work order of absolute proportions in this regard; it was incumbent upon the romantics, they announced, and part of the revolutionary surging of the literary absolute, to turn the literary into *work*, to hold literature and its fictional outlets to the standards of serious productiveness, to break away from reference yet transform the world poetically. The notion of productivity will have to be examined elsewhere, however, especially in terms of Nancy's *désoeuvrement* (idleness, inertia, being at loose ends) and the way in which "literary communism" de-produces the work.

*****

Regardless of the strained receptive stamina to which the "poor American" adheres, there's something to be said for holding the student position, the "*poor* student" as necessarily befuddled contender, unless one is condemned to the place of the disciple in *Faust*: Wagner, who lacks parricidal vigor or the surpassing dazzle of an ambitious younger scholar. Whether one has a handle on the way things go down, get filed or shredded or poetically shelved, the transmittal of an archive *is* unintelligible, in large part moved by an unconscious plate involving a spectral handover that relies for grounding on a widely illegible user manual.

*****

The objection raised to counter Cavell's trust in the philosophical merits of intelligibility – what he ascribes to the inheritable text – is not meant to come at him as an unwarranted intrusion, billed as a warning from outside his reflections. Precisely because *he* spotlights his mien as haunted receptivity in pursuit of the argument he feels compelled to make, naming a series of spectral blockages, his reflections, he intimates at the beginning of *Unapproachable America*, belong to the subgenre of *haunted writing*. The content onto which he attaches the attested condition or quality of being haunted (which, when spelled out, may prove to be contingent or may stand as a mere placeholder for another, nonthematizable level of traumatic erasure) may be, in the end, a matter of indifference. Even so, he flags a voided space to indicate that there is something that cannot be accounted for in his account, or philosophically demonstrated. The troubled state of haunted impoverishment, a drag on critical certitude and futural scheduling, requires a reading beyond evidence or thematic summation, at the edges of subjectivity and object formation, skirting yet priming history. Doubled, the spectral urgency that Cavell signals springs in him from the ambush of texts that hold a key to the self-dispersion caused in thought by the approach of the unapproachable, a hauntedness, crypt formation, the effect of the phantom contained in other works that he names, untouchably recalcitrant – athematic intrusions that disrupt argument and slow the rounding off provided by mathemes. All in all, Cavell's America is goaded by spectral uneasiness, a paracognitive field, though alien ("unapproachable") in nature and yet familiar to philosophy. There is a special bridge reserved for the convoy led in the past by Kant and Freud that returns strongly in Cavell's reading of Emerson's "Experience" and Thoreau's *Walden*. Since Kant, philosophy has been receding in grief, attended by phantoms – both acknowledged and still concealed – as it explores the limits of what we seek to know of and as the world. Besides his explicit considerations of a world visited by ghosts, Kant, on a differently tilted scale, in *Critique of Pure Reason*, is responsible for a conception of "the world for us" and simultaneously "of a world of experience denied or lost to us," inviting an understanding of how the world executes its withdrawal, holding a space for the unknowables. If our task lies partially in "recuperating," "such as we can," things and matters that lie beyond our knowledge, "then philosophy has to do with the perplexed capacity to mourn the passing of the world," avers Cavell.[18]

*

If anything, "America" will have inherited a European relation to loss that is framed by impinging worldlessness, even before European thought appropriates itself to itself. *Walden*'s emphasis on mourning and grieving, "as if grief and grievance are the gates of ecstasy," succeeds in "manifesting philosophical writing as the teaching of the capacity for dawning by itself showing the way of mourning, of the repetitive disinvestment of what has passed."[19] Philosophy is charged with offloading attachment by means of exemplary mourning and consistent shakeouts of "what has been formerly loved," as Nietzsche says, freeing up a relation to loss that detaches from the world, if not explicitly junking country, identity, and other vital historical attributes of material existence that must be renounced in order to affirm life.

*****

In order to press philosophy's task, Cavell turns first to Freud, who leads us to a hook for world-ing by means of a metaphysical glint, that of beauty recovered: "According to a reinvestment of interest in its discovery, something Freud calls beauty. (The pertinent Freudian text here, even more directly than 'Mourning and Melancholia,' is 'Transience' [1918])."[20] Something happens in the elaboration of Cavell's argument, a brief interlude flashing on grief, threading through Freud's bestowal of the beautiful, an interlude that allows Cavell access to the distinction he discerns in Heidegger between "clutching" at and "grasping" the world and, on the other hand, "being drawn to things" – between modalities of compulsion and modalities of attraction that mourning induces. He does not delve into the haunting disorders that compel Freud's attention or the anticipation of cryptonymy. Recoiling from the theme of grief, Cavell cuts away quickly, refuses to linger, saying only "I cannot presently deploy that fascinating material," and retreats with nearly military precision ("deploy") both from grief and from beauty.

*****

Instead of deployment, then, he defers to two women philosophers who have discovered, each singularly, Emerson's "awfully adept" way of "incorporating and denying the deaths (of wife, of brother, of son) he has had to absorb."[21] "Professor Sharon Cameron" and "Professor Barbara Packer" are brought into play. (I assume that the title of professor arrives as a sign of respect, but the gentlemen under consideration don't bear their university titles when called up in this work. *Peu importe* – no matter; one might take an off-ramp to study this allegory of sexual difference in grief, and anyway Hannah said more or less that the status of women in philosophy is lamentable – so, no, she does not consider herself a philosopher, thank you, and in the end "Professor" may turn out to mean that you are not really a philosopher, much less a *thinker*.) The "important recent engagement with Emerson"[22] conducted by the two sponsored women has pointed Cavell to grief that underlies his own work – grief contained by Emerson and gesturing on a nonthematic register, but already hiding out in the starter word "Waldo," an inherited family

55

name and that of his unmournable son; this name traveled all the way to the other in Walden, where the "wal(l)" of Emerson's transferred crypt crumbles. The son of Emerson, buried in his text under a sliding signifier, is not forgotten. Cavell's appreciation of the interpretive repair is unambivalent, if swiftly disposed of, once he has been reminded by the women professors of his own grief, estranged.

*

Basing his conclusions on Professor Cameron's elucidation, Cavell henceforth understands "Experience" to fall into the category of a work of mourning. Since he embeds Abraham, Torok, and Derrida in this work, we are handed instructions on how to read mourning, even if he himself refrains from so doing. He may want someone else, perhaps a *poor* American reader, to do the work of mourning for him. A surrogate mourner could make the loss intelligible and somehow keep the undeployed link to an extended Austro-French connection. Given the reluctance to mourn on the doubled parts of Emerson and Cavell, I would argue, however, that it is precisely not a *Trauerarbeit* (work of mourning), since the

Trauer (mourning) is stuck, unmoveable, and encrypted, but part of a stubborn mourning disorder that hangs on to the dead by dispelling the death deferred. All the same, the motif of mourning is crucial insofar as, for Emerson, mourning has a founding lever on the political, saying something about the American reluctance to count or cut one's losses. Yet mourning remains problematically sealed off, both for Emerson and for his commentator. What is it that keeps the phantom agitating, a living dead – an undead whose status cannot be adjudicated? I, too, refrain from treading further, even at the risk of crashing against the walled-up secrets of the Waldo wreckage. Cavell is clear about not wanting to delve further. If this were another sort of study, one would investigate how and why the philosopher halts, precisely here, wondering what prevents the close up and how this aversion affects his text, which is custodially handed down on this point to the women guardians reigning over grief and the unburied. This line of inheritability, a kind of mise en abîme of his project, where it feminizes and wails, walls, "waldos," may teach us something about the status itself of philosophy as it tends to its elusive object, an "America" slipping by in wordless grief, calling upon the experience of philosophy to detach us from doomed worlds, bringing on poetic starvation and summoning the lucidity of Freud for the purpose of retrieving an imago and a partial memory tap of a libidinized "America," furtively cathected onto its mourning disorder.

*****

Cavell himself finds in German thought and in the tradition of French critical rebuke a redemptive quality of world retrieval beyond a Spenglerian attitude of censure and disgust that he provisionally locates in *What Is Called Thinking?*, where Heidegger is at pains to back off from "what he calls Spengler's pessimism": an attitude, explains Cavell, "directed to the drift of one's culture as a whole that evinces radical dissent from the remaining advanced thought of that culture," an attitude that would "not make Wittgenstein unique among writers such as Montaigne and Pascal and Rousseau and Emerson and Nietzsche and Freud." Wittgenstein, different from his predecessors in timing, mood, and manner, capable of embracing the poverty of philosophical language, "comes from the sense that he is joining

the fate of philosophy as such with that of the
philosophy or criticism of culture, thus displacing
both – endlessly forgoing, rebuking, parodying
philosophy's claim to a privileged perspective
on its culture, call it the perspective of reason
(perhaps shared with science); anyway forgoing
for philosophy any claim to perspective that goes
beyond its perspective on itself. This is the poverty of perspective. But what makes this poverty
philosophy?"[23]

*****

At this point, bearing up under the pressures of
poverty and tenacious self-emptying, a kind of
philosophical kenosis, Cavell turns to Derrida
and Lacan, tendering an ambivalent embrace.
There is a misreading (and retraction) of *deferral* on whose particulars I must defer, because
it implies an infra-philosophical squabble that
would incite another dossier-opening gesture
when we want to stay put, limiting ourselves to
weighing in rigorously within the parameters of
American modalities of loss and the flex of self
loss as part of a national crypt formation to which
we shall return shortly. Tempted by Derrida's

and Lacan's metaphysical cutbacks and phantom nations, Cavell comes across "these findings of losses and lost ways, this falling and befalling" in Emerson and Thoreau, as he not only reads the loss of a child in "the idea of a child as founder"[24] – another emblematic effusion of the New World anthropomorphized, a breakaway from Wordsworth – but skids off the tracks of mourning as he sets out toward the unapproachable object, what he wrests from "America" as failed philosophical conquest.

*****

During a supplementary run through, a red flag appears when Cavell, as if picking himself up from unresolved mourning disturbances attended by conceptual shortfalls, tries to make a pitch for a full-bodied philosophical future. Unlike Nietzsche's "philosophers of the future" who roll in another direction, Cavell sets his mind to cheer on the philosophical resolve, skating on poverty in America, rebounding elsewhere. He may see a necessity in backtracking or embracing repression when planning to leap forward, thus leaving a strong margin of hope for posterity. It is not clear whether the short encounter with grief is to be left in the dust or is to behave as an ecstatic stimulant, following the suggestion of an earlier statement on Thoreau. Here is where Heidegger comes to the rescue, as it were, reinstalling the nexus of call and response, whether issued or withheld, but accorded by a more upbeat, Cavellian tonality. "Virtue" reopens a gate, however slightly, just enough to let succeeding generations in, readjusting the extent of a philosophical capacity to answer a call. Philosophy's "virtue is responsiveness. What makes it philosophy is not that its response will be total, but that it will be tireless, awake when the others have all fallen asleep. Its commitment is to hear itself called on."[25]

*

I like this mission statement; I think I'm on board with and motivated by its overall setup and insomniac edges. I even like that philosophy hears itself called upon, as part of a commitment made or in the making, to heed a policy of auto-affection ("hears itself called"). Nonetheless, I have some reservations about the efficacy and soundness of the statement's aim, given the way a recuperative operation crawls into philosophical headquarters at this point, presumably in order to secure a future or dust off a work and bind a philosophical project to the conditions for potential legitimacy. I'll just offer an insinuation of counterpoint, which understandably requires greater expanses when considering the limits of philosophical intervention – and certainly when assessing what kind of mourning disorder gets swept under the rug, an order of thought relegated to the offices of our philosophical ladies, as philosophy clutches at the future. In some instances the boldness of fast-paced responsiveness offers an advantage in terms of apparent resolve and ethical tensing, a necessary vigilance on the part of philosophical probity and tentative setup. Yet I am not sure that philosophy can or should be on the ready in the mode of first responder or lasting conscious-ness ("when the others have all fallen asleep").

*****

Let me "count the ways" in which, historically, this impulse portends disaster – with the proviso, as said, that I like the galvanizing prod or primal heat of alertness behind such a conception of philosophical maturity. Regarding any number of levels of self-justifying impulse, including the compunction to reach for a modicum of legitimacy, one shouldn't trust it: the wake-up call, no matter how piercing in these times of intellectual drowsiness of all sorts, appears overconfident. That is to say, I am not sure about the implicit storyline when, staying up through the night of extreme distress, receptive to or assuming the authority of sounding the alarm, the philosopher sits, tensely keeping watch. Nor am I willing to place bets on our capacity, as a *Geschlecht* (race, species, genus), for rousing from the slumber of depressed bouts of numbness and dumbness, so prevalent in our times. Although Cavell himself is riding the crest of defeat, bearing up under conditions henceforth of unavoidable privation, too many pseudo-philosophers think that they have been called on when, in Kafkan terms, the call may be misdirected, or even psychotically misheard – if this calling is a matter of a *call* at all, whether taken or declined, dropped or connecting, assumed or projected. In Flaubertian terms, one may be arrogant enough to think that the call is meant for you to accept, hold and handle, forward, file, defile, muffle, or even initiate. It's been a while since a philosopher has presumed to answer the call or even decipher its destination, much less consider it a destiny. There are, to be sure, other instances, less primed, to which the philosophical attitude is more prone – including that of falling asleep at the wheel, or shutting off the cries of other worlds of care in the flick of an incurious drop-off. It is not clear that a wake-up call, the corresponding clearance of responsible responding, should suffice to harness philosophical answerability or to describe, without a frisson of suspicion, the *virtue* of so doing: the spur of such a shock is always close to a call to arms, susceptible to shadowing a fascist wake for thought. It jostles, rouses, punches out the receptor, delivers a violent jolt, as in Heidegger's disassembling *Stoß* (push), where it becomes undecidable whether one is whacked or caressed by Being, whether one is gathered up or dented, called or indicted – or, in Lyotard's lexicon, whether one is chafing under *mainmise*, a throttlehold so great that it eludes perception. At the same time, responsible assumption is what we strive toward, a stance respectful of the persecuted passivity cast in Levinas. Can a tensional structure be held in place wherein philosophy, at once weakened and lucid, renounces its relation to discernible alarm, often misappropriated or overplayed by a dubious team? One imagines the mournful duties of the cleanup crew, gliding silently over the grounds, dejected yet methodical, similar to the cleaning ladies who tend, in Kafka and Clarice Lispector, to the remains of *litter-rature*, with no illusion of juggling redemptive leaps of faith, yet too tired for Spenglerian pessimism or too streetwise for residual forms of prescriptive lucidity, no matter how tentative yet on point. I daresay that no one is more practiced (or adrenalized) in the disciplined torture of catching a break or waiting for a call than a certain *We, the People* inscribed in the American breakout.

*****

In the past few centuries the themes of slumber, dozing off, and debilitation due to sheer exhaustion have been tapped. In the *Castle*, when K. is about to receive a revelation concerning his status, he falls asleep, shifting to a mode of non-presence that closes off any kind of substantial reveal. Even the unconscious receptor in Kafka appears to take a snooze, missing out on the messaging to which in principle he is privy. By the time Blanchot's turn comes, weariness is du jour, and the energy supply of thought barely holds out against the heaviness of metaphysical exhaustion. On the edge of extreme tiredness, two inter-locutors drag along in the allotment of meager resources available to them, perhaps rejoining here the earlier motif of impoverishment or running out the clock of philosophical vibrancy. If there were some perky way of announcing philo-sophical discovery in diminished times, it would no longer amount to a robust, if aphonic, call, a sacred instruction sheet, or a push for an edifying treasure hunt, even if the pursuit should involve, as in Kant, a firmly placed setting within the sober limits of philosophical capability.

*****

In the late sketches of Lyotard as well as in Deleuze's essay on Beckett, exhaustion leads the way to another experience of lived time, scraping bottom somewhere between consciousness and its others, where experience quenches in over-work and empty address, more or less voiding the bounce that takes us beyond good and evil and leaving one stranded with tiresome truisms,

pseudo-observation, and worn-out announce-
ments. One is, moreover, rendered sick and
tired by the pounding rhythms of *Chockerlebnis*
(shock exposure) – the allotment of hits taken,
whose disruptive consistency compromises the
very experienceability of experience. It is not
clear that we should *want* philosophy to recharge
itself, if this means reinstituting a false profession of sovereignty, revving up again a rhetoric of
promise and figures of transcendence, reclaiming
falsifiable premises, and driving us insane with its
righteous hold on "ethics."

*****

Well, some of the facets of the philosophical assertion have clocked out by now. Conducted off
the stage of its greatest vitality, in the exhaustion
of promises spelled out by Levinas and Nancy
among others, *philosophical fatigue* coincides with
the predicament of an "America" that has cut its
promissory engines. What are we to make of this
entity, as a rule feisty and presumptuous, endangering, posed as insubstantial facticity, at once
law-making and rogue, perilously self-assured,
uncontrolled, and void? If anything, the way

"America" runs itself down on empty – which also gives it a desperate edge – flags a condition that should encourage and enrage the "*poor* student" to search out the mourning disorder that triggers much of the overwrought action of the agitated, overeating, narcotically stuffed nation and that of its reciprocally cast, coerced, differently strapped partners, skidding into their post-ideological swap meets in Europe and "the rest of the world" (a syntagm criticized by Derrida). If the over-reach that Cavell saw in the romantic dream of philosophical and poetic suturing means some-thing today, or can teach us anything, it could be indicated in the sounding of an exigency – in the task of becoming *question-worthy* (*fragwürdig*, "questionable") (Heidegger, Lacoue-Labarthe, Sam Weber, Fenves), of becoming rigorously self-questioning, without relinquishing a stance of uncompromising *upset* (Paul Celan).

*

So. Stomaching insult and rundown, how do we stay in ongoing conference with the revolted (in the sense given this tortured word by Camus), where one goes toe to toe with what is *revolting*, upsetting historical tendencies toward repressed rewrites or coerced assimilation and false reparation? Perhaps we can continue explicating the predicament of brokenness according to different types of "unbelonging" (Paul Celan), scanning corners where "the caged bird sings" (Maya Angelou), revisiting the fateful turns that rotate out of Rome into New York, as the great cineaste Pier Paolo Pasolini projected them in *St. Paul* when contemplating the enduring sequels to the assassination of Martin Luther King, Jr.

Doch was heisst "fremd" (Mais que veut dire "étranger" [But what does "foreign" mean])?

Jacques Derrida[1]

Deconstruction and America are two open sets which intersect partially according to an allegorico-metonymic figure. In this fiction of truth, "America" would be the title of a new novel on the history of deconstruction and the deconstruction of history.

Jacques Derrida[2]

[1] Jacques Derrida, *Geschlecht III: Sexe, race, nation, humanité*, edited by Geoffrey Bennington, Katie Chenoweth, and Rodrigo Therezon (Paris: Seuil, 2018), p. 60.

[2] Jacques Derrida, *Memoires for Paul de Man*, translated by Cecile Lindsay, Jonathan Culler, Eduardo Cadava, and Peggy Kamuf (New York: Columbia University Press, 1986), p. 18.

2

The *Gestell* from Hell
A Lean Mean Fighting Machine

Holy *Unfug!*[1] Ranked for the most part as an outsider, Derrida completed his tour of duty in a way that is still unresolved. He nonetheless commanded authority as one who called the shots on the merits of a number of metaphysical strongholds still in service, trafficking unrelenting throes of injustice. On occasion, he was called upon to adjudicate unpopular standoffs in philosophical precincts, especially when theoretical scrutiny bled into politics. Far less prone than Heidegger to intruding upon the political stage, yet responsible to the moment, however frayed and delayed, Derrida, never forgetting the incalculable portion of rogue behaviors and the stray imponderables of terror, stayed alert to grievous acts of wrongdoing and calamitous downturns in social practices.[2] Confronting patriarchal privilege and its rotating recruits among institutional as well as remote-controlled onto-theological substructures, he chose his weapons carefully.

Jacques Derrida ran with the major downsizers of sovereignty, jogging a long-term memory of precepts and a foundation that destabilized our self-appointed sense of human dignity – a cut that stings to this day, inviting rollbacks and erasure, institutional forms of memory loss, distortion, wanton flip offs, secondary revision, and the return of subject privilege. Even so, when it came to calling out philosophically backed supremacies, he stuck to his guns.

Together with Freud, Derrida argues that it is still necessary to go back to our shared history in order to weigh the pressures of patriarchal overload, including the misogynist slams that have us all reeling, regardless of where we stand on the sliding scale of dominant forms of power. The disturbed endowment of the paternal throwdown, a prodigious source of power, has Freud saying in the end that something is amiss: we have yet to contend with the victory of patriarchy, notes the father of psychoanalysis. He puts it out there as if duty called, assigning a task not to be shirked, sounding an injunction. In this regard Freud joins Nietzsche when the latter doles out self-legislating responsibility – shaping something we *owe* ourselves to confront, an ongoing trial of thought by which we are tested and from which Derrida drew a number of critical lessons.

Derrida casts doubt on our capacity for welcoming an alien being, for throwing open an entryway without beating back the unrecognizable intruder – without screening the excesses of that which exceeds us, the blowup monstrosities, the different morphs of a beseeching other that shows up at your doorstep, or even our capacity to face down the terrifying angels announced by Rilke. The modern poet wondered in the *Duino Elegies* whether we could bear the endurance test of such an encounter, its lurking aggression: should an angel so much as approach me, *Ich verginge von seinem stärkeren Dasein* ("I would perish from its stronger being").[3]

Were something awesome to arrive, would we not crumble? Are we rigged to offer reception, or equipped in any way to sign for the event of awful consequence? Are we, as a *Geschlecht* (race, etc.) or mutant consort to beings and Being, capable of showing unconditional hospitality to the *arrivant/e*, the one who comes, releasing if necessary the maleficent raider in an act of pardon and awe? Regaining more earthly terrain: can one imagine a delivery of justice that supersedes the conceptual tethers of debt – the calculative penalty to mete out a just resolution of wrongdoing? In all these matters and on a wide range of related considerations or phenomenological sticking points, up and down the scales of Being and justice, Derrida stayed close to the bone of the aporetic character of our experience of indebtedness when tallying that which is due to others.

As oddball as this may seem in our day of urgent political collapse and faint recuperation, an overall grasp of Derridean codes of delivery alongside the concern articulated by the philosopher over misdirected missives and haunted sites will help orient our sense of the "destinerring" disruptions of democratic forms, part of a docket of *envois* (dispatches) left unprotected by any reliable logic of cognition or recognizable political theory.

There are critical times when democracy reroutes its stock of freewheeling itineraries by dispatching smart missiles or missives as part of a mission to "protect and maintain itself precisely by limiting and threatening itself." Derrida's argument emphasizes these "two contradictory movements of *renvoi*, sending off, that haunt and autoimmunize each other by turns." The democratic "ideal remains under a double or autoimmune constraint."[4] Democracy routinely has to knock itself out in order to prop itself up again and, in so doing, produces – or encounters and appropriates for the first time – its own field of enmity. Unleashing an "a priori abuse of force" by which "a democracy defends itself against its enemies, justifies or defends itself of or from itself, against its potential enemies," democracy comes to "resemble these enemies, to corrupt and threaten itself in order to protect itself against their threats. . . . The 'terrorists' are sometimes American citizens."[5] In a Benjaminian sense, the police are more ferocious in a democracy than in a monarchy.

The destructive send-ups by which democracy routinely tests itself, stresses and stretches itself, belong to the launch structure of a self-addressed envelope that continually pushes beyond its limits – one might say *beyond a civic pleasure principle*, to the extent that the democratic libido hitches a ride on the death drive, sent off to crash and burn, if it cannot pull back in time. The close calls and destructive jaunts on and for which democracy has been built – a consistent testing to failure, the exacerbating principle of its own deferral, and the promise of semi-resurrections – make it nearly impossible to tell whether democracy is the most robust or the most fragile of political bodies, beating out at every turn and trope the adversaries it attracts. Or, more simply formulated, does democracy not remain unavoidably bound for a shock of failure that it manages only for a time to avert, exhausted as it is by autoimmunitary contests? These contests are sometimes part of a civic thrill, a democratic daredevil's act of defiance in the face of unrelenting policing.

Against all odds, there is a moment when autoimmunity can be seen to strengthen up on its own depletion, building on nothing, aiming for its own vulnerabilities, playing to a defective cornerstone of democratic architectonics. The autoimmune impulse sends its own messages out to a body politic that it seeks to bulk and deplete according to a logic of self-protection and forms of security, prone to misidentification and chronic misfiring. Some of these paradoxes of autoimmunity that impinge upon internal politics are frankly Nietzschean, recalling Nietzsche's ability to pump up weakened states and bodies – or to counter the tendencies of pessimistic and Christian domination, where the meekest get to inherit the earth. Nietzsche is still trying to wipe the smugness from their resentful faces – a different project, though he does attack a kind of group psychology that characterizes "our democracy," as Americans like to say. In the meanwhile, democratic scenes of experimentation send themselves messages of protective urgency, strangely misdirected yet programmatically supported, as even the most permissive state – should such a thing exist (*was ist das? – ti estin?* – "What is it?" – Heidegger the Greek would ask)[6] – tries to invent and claim a national gathering point in the *We, the People* – a cluster that can turn poisonous at any bend or turn of violent national positing. The postal ballistics of immunization continually refresh national phantasms of safety and regulated social practice with punctual attacks on vulnerable alterities.

*****

Like Heidegger, yet coming from a different angle and historical sensibility, Derrida blew the whistle on democratic fragility, affirming it while calling out the inescapable fissuring of its defective cornerstone. Consequently, Derrida tries to prevent the looming foreclosure of democracy, seeking to preserve it as juridical and *literary* life form, prone to its own subversion and autoimmune crack-up. In fact Derrida opens a suicide hotline for the immunodeficient injury to which democratic life forms repeatedly succumb. Heidegger, by contrast, calls out democracy on the ground-level failures that foreclose futurity and invites "worldlessness." These are different fights, but they are fought on the same terrain, according to axioms at variance in a deadly clasp. Insofar as both thinkers saw the dangers associated with core survival issues linked to democracy as *task*, to drag Benjamin's translator into the fray – meaning as something we repeatedly give up on and accept as our gift, our burden, our *Aufgabe* – we need to bear the double and contradictory brunt of their vital insights.

*****

Heidegger's relation to place and emplacement, tied to remembrance and historial projection, breaches all sorts of political no-fly zones. His failures have been noted. Nevertheless, he saw and named the danger zone, still encroaching, if at times blinking in minuscule bursts. In his own emphatic way, Heidegger warned against the high-velocity expulsion of Mnemosyne, a kind of erasure and abbreviation that readily marks our deficiencies under the sway of the technological era. The American tendency to abbreviate proper names and titles was, according to him, a symptom of such a linguistic–technological reduction – hence the long list of acronyms and short types such as USA, CIA, PhD, DNR/DNI, CDC, SCOTUS, FBI, NYU, edtwt, lol, AI, and the like, fast and lazy codes crowding out a relation to language that hosts poetic and other complicated forms of saying.

Btw, it may be useful to indicate, though only by jumping a lane, that Heidegger's thought on forgetting and remembrance chooses not to enter the type of considerations made by Freud on distortion of memory, or on secondary revision and the intrusion of screen memories to cover the tracks on which recollection depends before derailing. Nonetheless, Heidegger instigates a grammatical disturbance by urging a gendered changeup in the neuter noun *Gedächtnis* (memory), which he rewrites in the feminine, *die Gedächtnis*. Of course, Heidegger's prod reminds us that we do have trouble remembering Being in any gendered or *Geschlecht*-driven form, but that's entangled in another level of forgetting, more invested possibly than Nietzsche's active forgetting or Plato's fast-track concerns with techno-oblivion.

*****

The internal political disturbances that the Americas expose cannot be limited to a simple though ongoing chronology of the Nazi era, some forms of which originate on the continent and feed Germanic voracity. Let us dig deeper.

Derrida shook down Heidegger with perseverance and care, patiently scanning for the very possibility of signs from a future as yet unknowable. Heidegger was vulnerable to his own stupidity, as he'd later say, setting up the

particulars of his hubris – the preposterous historical mythemes by which he was ensnared,
the metaphysical overdrive that, in or out of his
hands, turned murderous, his one big, "dumbest" mistake – carried off by nasty redneck
headwinds – of thinking that he *knew* which way
the wind of nationalist supremacy was blowing.[7]
At one point he applied to be the Führer's *Führer*,
expecting to teach and restructure a faltering
nation, riddled with vulgar self-evaluation. All
this is well-known, having been brought to light
by a number of active duty philosophers in good
faith, philosophical despair, and multiple rounds
of self-torment. Though trending and receding in
turn – tortured, troped and twisted by their own
abysses – philosophers of good faith that cover
recent catastrophic turns in thought and political
implication continue their probes as if our lives
depended on this work, obsessive and tireless, a
being-toward-death shaped by their stubborn feel
for questioning. Let us dig deeper.

*****

Apart from the odd standout, it was not always
fashionable for Europeans openly to embrace

America and concede the phantasms for which the land became a philosophical-poetic reception center. One made the occasional allowances for the importance of Ralph Waldo Emerson, maybe a nod toward Walt Whitman and the other one, Thoreau. By the twentieth century, the European language masters mostly signed on with Rilke's view that America represented an absolute void.[8] As a particular cut of a *We, the People* goes, Americans were stamped as *monstrous* by Rainer Maria Rilke (before the "ugly American" became an identifying feature of the greed-ravaged fellowship). The Austrian poet Nikolaus Lenau added fuel to that fire by noting, it could not be an accident that America hosted no nightingale in its ornitho-empirical birdscape – a missing element that amounted to a poetic curse on the land.[9] There would be no "Ode to a Nightingale" perching on some opiate drain – maybe only ravens and lunatics (or the screech of a crow in Jim Crow), swarmed by Hitchcock's menacing attack birds. Barren and consumed for the most part by raw greed, set for the advent of technologized tweets, America seemed bereft of poetic language, incapable of refined sensibility – and irremediably distant from the crowning song of a nightingale. Regarding the species, no one yet figured that the caged bird could sing.

Without starting a rumble, let me just point out that the gauntlet was thrown down over the *fate of poetry*, fostering an argument borne by an early European blindness to our American capacity for flourishing in the vacancy of a wasteland, if waste be the way to flag a startup essence of the American imago and cover the hard time put in penitentiary culture. – Before detailing prevalent types of aggrieved being, I hit the pause button. – Anyway, *excuse me*. Let me betray but one flicker of partisan poetics. Since when do poets feed off plenitude or indulge an opiate drawn from historical comfort zones? Or avert their gaze from landfill or from Paterson, NJ and other deficient national containers? Poetic gang wars notwithstanding, America was an object of ambivalent fascination by the time Derrida reappropriated, in and along his way, via Heidegger and the fields of German poeticity, what "America" could mean for the ends of philosophy, booking his tours with careful calibration and an eye for its vulnerabilities, concurrent theories of death and penalty, racial presumption and brutal zoning ordinances. America became, for a number of hard-core European thinkers, the proving grounds of ambivalent positing and ethical self-interrogation.

One of the common tropological markers of his day involved the *promise* of America, which at one point Derrida saw as constituting a state of, and in, theory. Taking off from his analyses, one begins to fathom a complex state of things, by which theoretical assertion and varied assumptions of powerlessness would be measured, being held at times to the rhythm and rhetorical scansion of fracture, disappearance, and return. Shaping a vision of American acts of promise, drawing on a frazzled horizon of the American dream to which the nation state has been consistently attached – as a push ahead, or intercepted by a kind of triumphal regression – the sense of what *returns*, even to newer states and corresponding proposition clusters, characterized Derrida's type of questioning: a relentless tracking of the revenant, a seeking out of that which comes back or threatens to do so, a looping Trail of Tears.

Yet what kind of purveyor of truth attaches to *promise* and *dream*, and how have these terms inflected and directed each other's political course in the New World? Can a dream be tested, or does it not open up to a deregulated scene of untried adventures from which one must soberly awaken? Let us ask differently, and again: to what extent does Freud's *Traumdeutung* (*Interpretation of Dreams*) help us protect America's dreamers? The question of state-bound dreaming and dreamers is as old as Metaphysics and the permits she oversees.[10]

Plato's integration of the dreaming citizenry became a point of disavowal for Freud, who refused to acknowledge a prior dream interpreter. As we have seen, the status of the dream in politics conflicted Plato, who did not want to see the nocturnal free-for-all blend into a politics of sunrise, cleared for political sobriety and lucid action, free of unconscious trespass, desire's imponderables, and parricidal frolic. The status of the dream in matters of political deliberation and wish fulfilment was crowded out by daytime negotiators who put constraints on the unruly spillover of dreams and the unconscious. Still, the intrusion of the oneiric state became a point of contention, an adversary and testing ground for metaphysically laden decisions and for the imposition of regulatory strictures. The law of the unconscious, already motivated in the *Republic*, was a bitter pill for lawgivers. From Plato's concerns over breakout dreamers to Rousseau's *rêveries* and beyond, dream streams flooded the political arena, testing the mettle of another force of law – divine, destructive, wishful, disorderly, underwriting covertly positing and outrageous behaviors among sleepers in the polis.

*****

The interruption of dogma offered by the dream, wedged in the *Republic* as promise and as irony of the promise, eventually morphed and migrated to America. Among other attributes and theoretical settings, America becomes a site for consistent reviewing; it requires backtracking and a registry of sudden growth spurts that involve political pain and blunders, a staggered effort to blend alterities and fall behind on a declaration of intention that was, from the start, compromised – and, according to stipulated revolutionary ground rules, contractually breached.[11] Yet there was something special about American exposures, the power outages built around a space, or an *Erörterung* (disquisition), where democracy ran

up a tab on continual testing, if it was not con-
ceived of as the very test site on which a modern
experimental wager is tried. On 9/11 the president
said: "This country is being tested." On January
6, the president said: "This country is being
tested." The second time around, the utterance
did not appear to assert that we had passed the
test imposed or that we had mastered a proleptic
trial run.[12]

To the extent that plaints such as "This is
no longer America" or "America has become
unrecognizable" have been recently multiplied,
especially by European monitors, one could hold
that America, primed on its instabilities, had
begun on this note and ceased to be, from the
start, *recognizable*, identical to itself. Or, shifting
to a dream rhetoric turned nightmarish, one can
observe another ostensible downturn. America
can no longer be seriously hospitable to idealiza-
tions about its dream currency. This is due in part
precisely to the inherent failures of the rhetoric
of promising – the different types of *(sich) ver-
sprechen* (promise, have a slip of the tongue) that
Heidegger, Derrida, Hamacher, de Man, and
others have analyzed, the peculiar mix of promise and misspeaking rooted in the German prefix

ver-. The ironic and reciprocal warps of promise and the American dream were repeatedly tested to failure following technological protocols and institutional snapping points, putting a restraint on daytime politics. At a juncture where technology meets its match in the rhetoric of dreaming, a nearly mechanical force of democratic resistance has been programmed to hit the limits of doctrinal pliability, repeatedly encountering a defective cornerstone on which democracy stands, falls, turns, teeters, collapses, recharges, rebounds, and depotentializes itself. Let me underscore here again, on repetition compulsion, that casting America within a literary space of dream and dreamers accords the very notion of nation an unconscious life stream, a logic that exceeds civic life restricted to material and politically based precepts of foundation or structuring principles. In her reflections on Freud and Plato (in that order), Sarah Kofman first detected Freud's suppression of Plato's dreaming citizenry and what happens to the polis when awoken to the daytime exigencies of political life. Under nocturnal cover, the Athenian (or rather Kallipolitan) citizen could romp with abandon, spring from the cages of regulatory compliance, though by daylight each and every one was called back to order, enjoined to straighten up, made to clear out the illicit accounts billed to nightfall. But dreaming does not necessarily conform to the diurnal clocking mechanisms of governance and legal prescription. The state of dream leaks and continues to stream, endangering with unbounded phantasms the ramparts of state and laws. Dreaming and blowing holes in narration, puncturing the girder meant to consolidate a citizenry, Plato's steely Kallipolis is placed on guard. For the entire edifice of just governance can succumb to the threat of collapse in one snap of the unconscious – a consequence of that premature discovery of Plato that was blocked out by Freud – according to Kofman's snapshot of their mimetic rivalry.[13]

Freud was not the only one to isolate and seal off unconscious resources ready to shake and take, or found, any state. The nightshift of Plato's and Freud's pooled citizenry unleashes all the demons, including those that goad incestuous pairings, bloodlust, and libidinal insurrection and are in league with those that prompt suicidal runs at the reigning taboo. It's not as though there existed a dependable off switch to shut down the unconscious release of depleting vampires and stateless spirits and a practiced troupe of destructive demonry. Repression cannot be expected to do the job once the sun comes up. Alright. *Asked and answered.* The prod of a fabulous poetry of slumber, ready to break down sober prohibition and reinforced barriers, is wielded by any philosophically primed republic that hosts dreams or is troped in the manner of dreaming. The country of dreams capable of dissolving repressive laws is also petrified by protocols of nightmare encroachment.

*****

The philosopheme "America," a theoretical petri dish by which I also mean to indicate, with referential consequence, a certain world-class bully that occupies the concept of "USA" (though, God knows, the Americas have also attracted other forms of dictatorship and have appealed to those stubborn "Germania" mythemes in forms and uniforms of a nationalist displacement and Nazi retrenchment; don't let the parenthetically shortened leash fool anyone; for this part of the argument, let us consider how European and American tropes reciprocally collapse, failing to maintain strict boundaries or secured separation clauses). Short of having Alexander von Humboldt lead the way to a strong modelling of investigative trekking in the Americas – he was looking for clues about origins that would offer Darwin a direct supply line for inquiry and appropriation, another thinking of the origin of *Geschlecht* – at this point I limit the focus of North America to the United States, where founding concepts of political arrangements are being stretched to breaking point.

It may seem odd to ticket Derrida and Heidegger on this terrain, asking them jointly – or disjointedly, in the spirit of *Unfug* – to reclaim America. The status of this land in reflections that press upon the fate of philosophy today remains tied to a class of repression, the effects of which threaten the globalized world every day. The philosopheme "America" is responsible for a number of uninterrogated sketches, different hypothetical assumptions, poetic jumping-off points, if not straight-out conclusions in works of thinkers whose legacy we continue to construct and swim with. Let us look now at the American launch in philosophical and literary works of the German language, beginning with Kafka's unfinished novel *Amerika*, which repurposes "America" as a kind of political theater.

From vaudeville antics to various vignettes that update (or would close down) Heinrich von Kleist's short essay "Über das Marionettentheater" ("On the Marionette Theatre"), Kafka's writing rides the signifier as a feature of the literary imaginary, taking "Amerika" from spectacle to the discourse network of intense medial output. America – as poetic poignancy or philosopheme, theoretical scaffolding, imaginary extension of a European province, or home to the technological masterstroke – appears of course in an abundance of other key works as well, many of which closely detail, like Kafka's, vacated spaces and abandoned props, a scattershot of objects on which to test and stage concepts of displacement or essential vanishing. You can plan a getaway or customize your dreams, you can enlarge a theater of quirky personhood, but be forewarned: people vanish in America; the gods have lapsed, fake IDs are routinely crafted to seal the deal of take-no-prisoners desubjectivization; death sentences prevail, to supplement the feats of death denial programmed by cultural institutions. At higher levels of state violence, putting to death as a penalty in pseudo-democratic circuits has always attached to a theatrical component, cranking the cathartic excitement of spectacle. There is far more to be said here, and others have created important discursive spaces that hold for review these morbid spectacles of surging injustice, so I will not rant or stoke anal–sadistic energies with which the state gorges a good conscience, but only gain on Kafka's startup text as a modelling instance. Entering "Amerika" via Kafka makes us boat past a Statue of Liberty that brandishes a sword in one raised hand, rather than a torch.

Freud picked up some conceptual props for his own version of the American experience when he imported to his thinking the figure of oversized trucks transporting homes – and the whole mechanism that rigs mobile homes, motoring recreational vehicles of the unconscious – to describe *displacement* in the case of obsessional neurosis. How Americans move their homes shows them capable of dislocating and rearranging the notion of "space" and, by inference, particular topologies of metapsychological import. Yankee ingenuity, mobilized and mobile, fixated on the vehicle, drivers, and drives, is used to affirm the deracinating grid of unruly self-exposure, a move that troubles the European tropes of rootedness that some American sectors have in the meantime adopted. Freud is less severe about manic displacement. He shows tenderness toward the American invention of the "flirt" able to flit and fly with libidinal flutter, an affirmation of unsteadiness that Freud does not castigate. Nietzsche would be on board with the type of superficiality revealed in libidinal grazing as well.

Not only did they kick aside ideologically set expectations that tout the reliability of soil and ground, but Americans as a *type* consisted of those uprooters who can up and leave on a dime: they can cue up departures, unstick themselves or scram, go anonymous, fleeing a crime scene, relinquishing the privilege accorded to some crucial tropologies of stay-at-home nationhood. Nietzsche, for his part and at the short end of the stick of stuckness, was watching the film of extreme mobility that characterizes Americans – and Jews without statehood – offering his approbation of the mobility he savored, of the dream of blowing up a station in life (whether by burdened necessity or whim or writing), of going for broke by a switch-up in identity, and of the ability to show disdain for false sovereignties, substance or ground, whether groomed by persecution or by the decision to be a Marrano, secretly harboring one identity while playing off dominant trends, as Derrida has repeatedly explained. Nietzsche – the champ of "moving on," of "getting over oneself" even as he was chained to the caprice of a pernicious sister like Elisabeth Förster-Nietzsche, the ruling anti-Semite of the Nietzsche household – was in many ways made in the USA. He was not unaware of the contradictory shortfall characteristic of a sovereign state staking itself on democratic values that are often no more than self-cancelling experimental wagers and, at best, the epic fails of earnest political tryouts and inevitable theoretical retractions. Nietzsche was also no stranger to what becomes Adorno's F-factor on the American scorecard – a cipher for the fascist potential inherent in American forms of democratic governance. Admittedly, I cannot state in good faith that he developed Adorno's thesis for him. Still, Nietzsche had America's number in terms of imagining another way of philosophizing, ambivalently powering through excessive historicizations, faltering, and dusting off monuments with a hammer. [§*Sidebar*] I would want to hear out Alexis de Tocqueville's understanding, and prediction, of the increasing *juridification* of relations in America, by the legal susceptibilities to which each encounter is marked from the start as proving vulnerable to prosecutorial scrutiny and corresponding allotments of punitive damages. In terms of the formation of a national crypt, de Tocqueville's predictions lead us back, if by indirection, to something that was revealed by the Donner Party's cannibalistic trek across America – a fit of munchies that provoked national nausea and spawned the technologies of condensed milk in addition to other remedial countermeasures, including the invention of food preservatives meant to keep us from chowing down on fellow citizens. This allegorical slice of history is meant only to show how Americans were at and *in* one another's throats, shocked by the disclosure of their own limitless capacity for predation – a startup for technological innovation, articulating the need for putting a lid on a national voracious tendency sublimated to law. Acts of destruction have distinct national flavors on the menu of depraved dispositions. In many ways, the Donner Party precedent of desperate transgression flags the emergence of the American version of *Totem and Taboo*, a founding feast distributing "bits and pieces" of the national body, a morcellated body made of morsels and remorse, trying to keep down a murder scene repressed – one of those hidden origins on which all sorts of unconscious liabilities must be henceforth tabulated. Americans keep a close watch on the festival of incorporation and have a habit of keeping the other close, if not undead. How else could one account for the promotion of the former enemy into a cathected national food fetish, the Hamburgers and Frankfurters, the uncontested hot dogs of any culinary race? [*StopSidebar*]

*****

On the eve of his collapse, Nietzsche wanted all anti-Semites shot. The outrageous exaction alone served to prove to Dr. Wille, the admitting physician at the Friedmatt psychiatric clinic, that Nietzsche had succumbed to madness. One will also find in the doctor's notes proof of Nietzsche's *Umnachtung*, mental collapse, namely that this patient, Mr. Nietzsche, claimed to be famous. When he was still making some sanctioned sense, Friedrich Nietzsche followed the fate of Americans and European Jewry, who, according to his perspective on breaking down the world and making it viable, knew all about creating the fiction of a presentable self, pitching his own pre-fab versions in *Ecce homo*. Let me indulge my own madness by means of another stroke of repetition compulsion, because, as a projective fiction, this remains "too good to be true" – Freud's favorite American locution. According to Nietzsche's calibrations, these chronic diasporic troopers, the Jewish blends – American, African, and Arab – a vanguard of the experimental disposition that Nietzsche prized, test out different adaptations, perspectives, and signature strokes, maintaining a position as historically tried risk takers. Basically stateless, they were spurred on by defiant boundary-breaking prompts that left fairly conservative identitarian schemes in the dust and created what Heidegger labelled, in terms of figuring another *Geschlecht*, the advent of the "transhuman," offering at the time an upsetting translation of Übermensch. It was Philippe Lacoue-Labarthe who brought to bear on these texts and those of Paul Celan the crucial value of the *upset* – or the philosophical tumble of *being upset* and the exigency of preserving *the upsetting* in, and by, poetic language usage.[14] As we have seen, Nietzsche knew how to stay upset and give philosophical transit to the upset stomach – Nietzsche, the great expectorator, ever reversing dialectics, throwing up Christian values as part of his thought on well-being.

Heidegger and Derrida pick up Nietzsche's transatlantic relays, starting out from the basis of American groundlessness. Reflecting, if not helping to *invent*, dossiers of our modern philosophical heritage, their preoccupation with "America" indicates diverging programs of self-appropriation and nationalist contingency – signaled, in some instances, by the misappropriations or *insubstantiality* for which Nietzsche stood and fell. [*§Sidebar*] Taking another lap, one would want to analyze against this backdrop the way Carl Schmitt and Alexandre Kojève dealt America into their theoretical portfolios, the latter casting Japan as a formidable counterexample – a nation state capable of breaking ahead toward a viable political future. According to Carl Schmitt, *Kronjurist des Dritten Reiches* (crown jurist of the Third Reich), the discovery of the New World is responsible for the origin of the Eurocentric global order. *The Nomos of the Earth* situates the United States, despite its egregious flaws, as the only political entity capable of adjudicating the crisis of global order. Carl Schmitt's political theories do not stop here. They return through legal US documentation in support of George Bush's justifications for acts of torture in the wake of

9/11 and in other scenes of terror, supplying rhetorical arms to the current right-wing takeover of the judiciary. [StopSidebar]

*****

Sharp as a proleptic whip, Nietzsche alerted us to the philosophical spot where, in Heidegger's overall considerations, anti-Semitism shades into a form of anti-Americanism. Nietzsche identified a specific flex that, when generalized to remarks by future fellow philosophers, continues to remain uncontroversial – not particularly anti-Semitic, just part of a hermeneutic given in the conflating worlds of theoretical exegetes and practicing philosophers: one is left *waiting* for a reaction to untouched speculations based on New World assumptions. Who has raised an objection to the stock of anti-Americanisms hosted by modern philosophy (except possibly Richard Rorty, when pointing an admonishing patriotic finger *at me*, a confirmed conscientious objector whose reproval of American violence had, in his view, crossed a limit)? This is a stance that holds its course consistently, but might deserve at the very least a pinch of critical ambivalence or interrogatory wonder. To be sure, "America" has shored up phantasms of hyperbolic *Weltlosigkeit* (worldlessness) in terms of the overdrive of capitalism that it promotes and a launch for nomadic technologisms, tropes problematically associated with modern Judaic trajectories. From the desecrating passages sprung open fairly recently from the *Black Notebooks* we learn that, for all intents and purposes, worldlessness means "Jews" in Heidegger – in sum, those targeted people who represent, in the contexts he outlines, the universal takeover of technology.

As for an infratextual corner I'd like to turn, I would indicate here that Heidegger's theoretical disdain for "America" parallels a blindness in the unfolding of his own thought, and this in at least two ways. If anything, "America" never made a serious pitch for originary unity or fourfold wedding plans. It could not boast a poet witness to name its friended proximity to the gods, unless Hölderlin were to come back, blitzed on acid and adopted by "Paul de Man in America," one of Derrida's themes. (The acid is not part of his stash, but a kind of philosophical stimulant, offered to Heidegger in Freiburg by Ernst Jünger, dropped by Foucault in Berkeley, and so on: Derrida himself was wary of drugs ever since opening Plato's pharmacy and after the setup he suffered for a drug bust in Prague.)

As we all know, Heidegger reserved tropes of gathering unity for the poetically retrieved phantasms of Greek "Germania," consistently underplaying originary disunity. Contrasting a perspective sponsored by Nietzsche, Heidegger's pet project would be put off by an "America" that consistently re-marks disunity, ironizing its cobbled name, the so-called *United* States, verging in critical times of conflict on coming apart.[15] Moreover – and this will seem like a stretch, since I cannot pledge enough pages to back up this hypothesis – "America" will have voided its future, a common enough theme, to the extent that, as a being, or even as a stroke of Being overgrown with the technological gridwork, it stands as a refutation of ecstatic or unified time. I will accelerate where I might otherwise issue a requirement to that part of me, philosophically cathected, to dig in and explicate: if we had time, we would want to study, according to the relevant registers of a pragmatic critique and theoretical stamp, how "America" shakes off a relation to time as that which is seized up in being-toward-death.

In short, I would want to apply a *Daseinsanalyse* (existential analysis) to the way "America" times itself, chronically outrunning the European clock. Subject to the nicks of another time zone, something is still ticking on the American beat of Heideggerian *Sorge* (worry). I grant the untoward cut, in more recognizably orthodox Heideggerian terms, that seeks to divide our time by the beats of a material continental difference. But such a scansion would not be that far off as I follow *his* cues when he dropped the ball in this court. Posing a problematic entry, "America," though still surprisingly young and untried, was seen by Heidegger and his interlocutors to close off the future. Fried by technological excess, the continent was also cushioned by the very technological bearing that belongs to the registers of failures marked in relation to death. Evacuating from its fold the very possibility of futurity, "America" still operates, however, as a revelation of Being. It is as if something perturbing about "America" could be overcome, returned to sender, like the technological exploit that his work in some ways seeks to tamp down, scraping against the absence of spirit, *Geist*-lessness. Breaking with the past "America" also suspends the future, blocking a way for Dasein. For, anticipating its death, Dasein's temporal structure flows back from the future.

In sum, the America cast by Heidegger looks away from "being-toward-death," technologically diverted from a first-level destruction that its media outlets nonetheless generate compulsively and that keep it part of a proud boyish swagger of gun culture, in lockstep with a persistent threat of war, whether surrogate or mano a mano. Death under erasure and the overproduction of thematically unleashed killing sprees amount to the same curve of representation, framing a specific Weltbild. (*But, please, get me out of here.* I leave a more extended *Daseinsanalyse* for another interpretation of our broken and reciprocally bound philosophical homelands, for some of Heidegger's America bashing belongs to a projective swerve from the storage space of Germania.)

*****

For our purposes, which are strictly limited to initializing the American search engine, I have had in mind only to open a dossier, however unmasterable, in the hope that future researchers may drop into the probe of "America" as object of speculation and incorporation, to include the works of many others who have migrated with their tremendous baggage of persecution, dream, determination, reinvention, crushing history of self and other, conflicted appropriation. I would want to list and enlist all of them, with the understanding that cutting back on such lists – an ultimately wrongheaded but in some ways necessary decision – requires and deserves instead a monument to hold these names, all the names of this history, scanned, archived, maligned, forgotten, or "Americanized" on Ellis Island. For now, let the singularities of exilic wanderers provide a small indicator of those whose work and material displacement were inflected by a collapsible *eidos* (form) of "America" as destination, putting in place a destiny drained, for the most part, of mystified grounding. In times of despair – ask any immigrant – a pop-up destiny will do.

*****

It may be true that "America" and Heidegger shared a tendency before they split. Both entities seem bent on assigning a self-originating source, a destinal impulse, by rolling back to the Greek world, cleaving to the classics. On the way to language, they bypass Europe, and in one case bank on a classically instigated mania, that of "Germania."

*****

The philosophical relatedness of old Europe to the break-off point called up by the American dream and by Nietzsche's projections indicates for us how differently Heidegger and Derrida rode the signifiers organized around the American-dream text of ideological diversity, its nightmare edges, and its democratic self-comprehension. The decision, in George Bush's days, to corner the term "Old Europe" (announced in 2003 by US Secretary of Defense Donald Rumsfeld) primed Europe for renewed generational contestation and parricidal attack, a relation conditioned on the expulsion of Mnemosyne and her archive of adhesive memories. The tepid recollection requiring a European background check, delivering an incessant questioning of a broken origin, fires up a rapport to that ambivalently drawn origin, a disavowed matrix and an irrecuperable past. *[§Sidebar]* What I am identifying as "America" and "Europe" is two entities continually on each other's case, reviewing unconscious protocols for opting out or staying in the game of impossible relations, resetting the global North and colonialist holdouts, singing in tune to the ontologically adapted lyrics, "Is You Is, or Is You Ain't My Baby?" (flip side of the recording "G.I. Jive"). *[StopSidebar]*

The reciprocal readings bounce off the cabled continents and help us situate how German philosophy and adaptive cultural habits, whether acknowledged or dissimulated, turn to "America" not only in the rush of so many theoretical projectiles but in order to assess something about Germany's fabled self-constitution and historical evasions, some of which cannot be redirected, faded, or definitively resolved. If Nietzsche and Kafka imagined a hermeneutic horizon for *Amerika* that exceeds hermeneutics – a circularity of concept and trajectory, a pre-given understanding – this was also, of course, in order to find, beyond mere congruencies, a force strong enough to contrast with Europe, a force capable of providing an outright break with Germanic phantasms of statehood that, ever since the Goethe period (*Goethezeit*) and its predecessors, tended toward unity, sponsoring a concept of oneness that sought to secure the essence of Germanity, *Deutschheit*, in language and thought – a national entity that could not be partitioned or shared, auctioned off or blended. Impeaching such mystifications, Nietzsche liked American crack-ups and the license taken with willed fragmentation – an offshoot of what becomes known as mementos of rugged individualism, historical shredding, broken familialisms, and attendant shooting sprees, trigger points for brooding isolationism. Nietzsche's breakthrough dissidence showed us that "America" could and did resist a key Germanic temptation for a while, warding off a tendency that culminated in projecting on historical stomping fields an *essential Deutschland*.

I understand that I'm fast-tracking my hypothetical assertion, which chiefly has German idealism, associated with a facet of its Heideggerian uptake, mirror the American dream fragment, its nocturnal cover. Lobbed across the Atlantic, the Germanic phantasm resurfaces in different sectors of the American wilderness, with distinct theoretical bolsters. But I cannot widen the scope to cover the many prongs of encroachment that the returns of German "idealism" portend for us today, including that of the primary 9/11 pilot, Mohamed Atta, who was trained in Germany – a student of architecture, fearful of flying.[16] If we could follow the projectiles both of Heidegger and of Derrida on some of these points of departure alone, we would have to concede the send-offs and diverted destinations that travel to this day between the philosophical stakes in "Germany" and "America," often held over according to unconscious protocols and velocities, delivering barely managed parts and gusts of repressed historical memory. Bearing in mind Freud's accelerated press on the death drive, we adopt what psychoanalysis also sees as an *Aggressionstrieb* (aggression drive).

Let me continue to narrow the frame and make it manageable, before we set our sights on another missile–missive sent over from Germany, in the form of an immigrant family that could not turn around when it wanted back in, getting dissatisfied with the rough edges of a predatory America. This would be the story of the Trumpf family, another German gift, shaved off the *Aggressionstrieb*. The immigrant family, expecting to find its match in a uniquely American capacity for brutality, couldn't hack it: the unredeemed return ticket to the German homeland is part of the history and sending of Being, a fold in the *Geschick des Seins* (destiny of being), so much so that every send-up, no matter how derisory, backlogged, or anthropologically set, can come off, like technology, as a dent or fateful accident – a revelatory hit in the *Geschick des Seins*. Close to the contingent hit of race, as coup or chance, discussed in Derrida's *Geschlecht III*, the burble of chance events proves to be part of our *Geworfenheit* (thrownness): a crack in *being-thrown* that can become unavoidably decisive.

*****

For now it is important to acknowledge that the projections of old Europe on *Amerika* – or *l'Amérique* – do not travel only one way but become absorbed and returned, if by deflection and distortion, no matter how purportedly numb or dumb or indifferent to the European philosophical invasion a cross-Atlantic relay may prove to be. American dibs on legendary ignorance bespeak a strangely receptive openness, which gets shut down periodically but is none-theless more bloated with foreign influence than anything European (except when Europe is on a colonialist rampage, aggressively hugging an old map). The locality of *influence* is another matter. In *Wings of Desire*, director Wim Wenders offers that *die Amis* (the Americans) have "even colo-nized our unconscious," displacing the topology of invasive resettling. Heidegger, who has never been to America (or Greece, for that matter), seems to use these force fields as material refer-ence, at most an empirico-theoretical outpost of *Gestell*. Derrida, who booked hundreds of round trips, adopts more Nietzschean parameters, in addition to rhetorical as well as textual–historical instances – beginning with the temporal violence responsible for the very invention of the United States. In the flavor of "declarations of independ-ence," he identifies a haunted undecidability that shapes *Mémoires*, consolidating numerous analy-ses of 9/11, over-the-top professions of faith and religion, the breakdown of sovereignty in face of worldwide protest, representations on American television of obscene wealth in addition to patiently archiving texts treating law, history and temporalities of foundation.[17] Moreover, here

in "Déclarations d'indépendance" Derrida ana-
lyzes the violence *and* the invention of America
largely in terms of (a) the backstabbing flips of
performative and constative statement and (b)
the rhetoricity of self-appointment.

Still, despite the intelligence barriers, some
thoughts flying in from European capitals have
stuck. In the last US elections, the phobic anxiety played out against European socialism proved
to be a deployable prod, if only to wash out the
residue of communist giants. The spectral stalk
of communism has always seemed to be heading
our way when it comes to recurrently prosecuted
socialist trespass, the red threat.

*****

In their coproduction, Rilke and Heidegger
also put a spectral stamp on America, reviewing the ghostless housing plans, putting a block
on Freud's reception of mobility, but picking up
on similar characteristics that have New World
dwellers unmoored, going with the flux and
flow of desolation – a flow that has obscured
hearth and coziness in their own housing units.
American homes were seen by the poet and by

the philosopher as dangerously ungrounded, exposed and emptied of the haunted cushion of spectral ancestry. No one lives there any more, particularly not the dead. The endless suburbia of uprooted vacancy left Heidegger and Rilke queasy, while America, under firm technological sway, proved to be uninhabitable, or at least without the spectral cover of history. These observations continue to indulge the view that America has "no sense of history," a point of freedom that Americans tend to fuel up on at moments of manic *Selbstbehauptung* – the body bump of untimely self-assertion – a freeing up that Nietzsche savored on one of his pages of contradictory profession, before turning the page.

When sizing the overburdened relation of the European to a history that weighs on weary nationalist shoulders, the last philosopher, Friedrich Nietzsche, saw an answer in the American capacity for rapid self-mutation and round-the-clock restart. Let me state again that I struggle with the reductive temptation to pit Nietzsche against Heidegger on this front, egging on an implicit confrontation with what constitutes a land or a fatherland, the Blut und Boden strife, part of a grim history of thought that Nietzsche, a priori and on paper, discarded along with his ID cards. For, in the first place (if one can stabilize "place"), Heidegger made reluctant accommodations for being-not-at-home, a technological switch that also scores a moment in the revelation of Being. I have tried to follow his logic of *Gestell* and technicity elsewhere, remembering that he considered the *Technik* sector of his thought the greatest contribution he had signed, an essential handout and legacy warmer. While that path did not lead nowhere, *Holzwege* (*Off the Beaten Track*) style – he had a thesis to defend, an historical goalpost to breach – the question concerning technology held its line as a *question*, remaining part of a *Ge-spräch* (dialogue) that repelled a quick answer, and kept its dead spot intact.

*****

The pileup of Germanic tropes in the Trumpf era – the accumulation of geo-archival memory taps, and even, more broadly, the jokingly stated fact that *nowadays* one has been fleeing to Germany whereas in *those* days one was fleeing to America from Germany – should possibly not be left to some scholarly sidebar. Or am I mistaken?

Scholars have endured their degradation on a number of registers, which is why at one point, against his own grain, Nietzsche gives them a shout out, appreciating their parched deserts and dusty philology.

Scholars under the regime of Trumpf have been a targeted species, disdained and marked for controlled extinction. I will defend them, even if the feelings are not always mutual and I myself have struggled with the university as an autoimmune lab that kills off its own kind. At the same time, yes, the university lends out its premises *at times* as a sanctuary for existentially diminished souls; it has housed dissidents, bookworms, and queers like no other institution of waning solidity. I will refrain from switching on the history channel that features deplorable episodes – ethical lapses ascribable to university life, racist installations despite affirmative action inlays of yesteryear, ego-driven privilege, rectoral dereliction, bureaucracies on the prowl, and so on. In its time of political diminishment and moralizing overreach, the university nevertheless remains, in the eyes of its pupils, a necessary shelter for all kinds of divergent claims and intentions. It is not clear whether the university will revive after the knockout punch served by pandemic and political scarification, an entire generation's precarity, the choking out of professors by time and trend, the distortion of their legacies – it is not clear what all this destruction means and portends.

*****

We have seen how Nietzsche valued, in the very idea of "America" in his scattered writing, the bounce of its insubstantiality, a rapid-fire skill in self-adjustment when it comes to shifting ground and mystifications of identity. He understood that any identitarian urge, no matter how laudable and courageous in times of steadying imposition, stems from fear, if not from mimetic freefall. It is not easy to stand one's ground when conceding groundlessness. When the democratic experiment falters, it caves in to fear and phobia, hardening on the language of essential self-gathering, feeding in desperate moments on tropes of hardy selfhood.

A question remains as to whether the syntax of state emergence is a matter of pen or sword, or, if it cuts both ways, where the two might cross. It is arguably the case that *any* rally around usable precepts of recognizable identity has fear as its birthmark, which is not to discount persuasive aspects of liberatory self-assertion that rely for survival on mystified forms of group coherency. An empty call to originarity, Make America Great Again (MAGA) has inscribed repetition and failure as its principal markers, depending as it does on artificial nostalgia ("great again") and the fiction of a return to lost ground. In "America," the felicitous production of fakes has quickly become an accelerated side hustle, a national sport. At some point, perhaps, given the posited shrewdness about feats of nonoriginarity and rapid changeover, national *disidentification* becomes the rule – a familiar practice prescribed by Nietzsche in an entente with Emerson, emphasizing the countdown of his studied deauthorizations and personal detachments. Coming from team Nietzsche and the American philosopher, such a practice can go both ways – or, in Derridian parse, it can be said to come "both/and" ways. The ability to keep ditching former identities is known to involve a stock of unwieldy trade-offs, rhetorical ploys of power that feed on audacity by remastering a lexicon of nationalist pride with fake Christianity and other value shells. Nietzsche took it a step further. He detected a recurring structure in the triumph of bold-faced distortions, a flex of the will to power, as one of the programs that run through American scenes of destructive break-downs and seditious impulse. He saw mendacity, which could come from pessimistic quarters, but also from *life-affirming* impulses; and he did not shy away from destructive outcomes that the will to fiction and fakery implies. At the same time, one must acknowledge the abiding structures at play, including what Derrida sees in his work as the dependency of any call for originarity on a structure of return, even if this requires for its basis a falsified source. The "again" lodged in "great *again*" is part of a ghostly retrieval system that calls upon the revenant, no matter how voided the origin or how fake the claim.

Let me risk an overreach. There is unques-tionably something Heideggerian about calling forth a renewal of greatness, hidden or forgotten, stifled as an undertow of Being. A mythically revived "Germany" was also the birthplace of democratic governance – however flawed and partial classical Greek democratic forms proved, however planted in self-perverting hyperbole.

While fueled by the fervor of appropriative privilege, Heidegger builds forgotten Being on foreign shores, philosophically seized, and under the penalties of historicity, as he seeks the Greek origin.

The *Schlagwort* (catchphrase) MAGA shares a similar impulse of calling up a lost, if photoshopped, plenitude (I simplify for effect), but suspends the reference and collapses on the overdraft of its self-identical positing. For what is constituted in this rhetorical conjuration of greatness recalled? Following different routings that continue to bypass devastated crash sites and desolate flashbacks, *die Wüste wächst!* ("The desert grows!") sirens up from Nietzsche's pages.

[*§Sidebar*] Are we dreaming?! I remember the scandal of Ali's performative dare, "I am the greatest!" *But when exactly, and for what duration, was America great?* – one may ask of Mnemosyne, in the corridors of speculative thought. As a dream, yes, maybe. [*StopSidebar*]

*****

The catastrophic twentieth century called on a specter of greatness from "America," shaking out European maps and alliances, preparing the occupation and economic *Wunder* (miracle) of a partitioned Germany. Some French conscriptees scrambled to Freiburg to grab philosophy lessons. Others, sons of military officers such as Jean-Luc Nancy, grew up in Allied-occupied military zones, as children pickled in the German language and wearing lederhosen. My uncle, Daniel Penham, was a professor of French at Columbia University and was heavily involved in the denazification of the German university. He sifted and sorted through endless dockets. The longest interview or interrogation he recorded was with Karl Jaspers.

*****

Hélène Cixous contemplates Derrida's ironic embrace of America, scoping the formidable reception area it has provided for deconstruction. Writing about Derrida's Americanization in relation to his thought on "God, circle, volt, revolution, torture," she concedes:

> You know that he put (himself) America to the question by tormenting himself, etc. I thus note here, leaving it pending, that the first of the four algebraico-comical-pseudo-definitions of Deconstruction that it amuses him to wave about is

(1) Deconstruction is America. It amused him to say this . . . a little like saying it's a dream, you've hit the jackpot, it's Eldorado, it's the end of the world. It's not by chance if this very religious, hegemonic, but fragile country offers Deconstruction a scene, if not a battlefield or a field of privileged confrontation. Deconstruction happens naturally; it has no frontiers. Why not say: Deconstruction is Europe?[18]

Cixous imputes a mood of oneiric positing to Derrida when saddling America with deconstruction. One also assumes that he was wide awake and dead serious when drawing up complicated drafts about what could be expected from the ungovernable hypothesis, an "America" that is by no means a natural entity for Derrida, nor merely limited by its ever imperializing frontier zones, but something principally supported as a field of thought in strife – haunted and haunting, spilling over its boundaries in yet to be discovered ways, and at once threatening, though too disjointed to anticipate or stabilize. No one in her right mind would try to round up the entity "America" into a unifiable concept or ride it toward a recognizable horizon. At the same time, one cannot deny that it bears witness to and continually re-implements institutional and conventional markers that function to justify such a fragile unity. [*§Sidebar*] For our immigrant parents, destitute and needing to build a good object, "America" offered a way to introject greatness and subsist on a promise – supplied by an often wobbly rhetorical life raft. After all, to stick with our slice of world, Europe was a killing ground; one couldn't even scrape by the ongoing death penalty that it mercilessly delivered to the internally unwelcome and maligned. [*StopSidebar*]

*****

In his seminar on nationality and philosophical nationalism, Derrida points out that the humanist sequence of German national philosophism, reappropriated by Nazi ideologues, was made in the name of a *Lebensphilosophie*, a philosophy of life, even where life was understood only as spiritual life.[19] The establishment of the German language as sole custodian of a primary philosophy after the Greeks troubles Derrida, who sends up a warning flare. Beginning from Fichte's theoretical expansions of a German pride invested in *Deutschheit essentielle* (essential Germanity),

Derrida refers us to a Germanity more originary than any empirical traits could account for.[20] To the extent that Germanity sees itself as a crucially alone-standing philosophical power, it needs to protect itself against contamination from any foreign incursion. The more primal the asserted primacy, the more immunodeficient the national entity – and the more prone to invasive compromise. The twist in Fichte's argument occurs when the mark of foreign intrusion comes from *inside* a nationally bound entity. There is thus, wedged in Fichtean nationalism, a pernicious cluster of "fake Germans" who mangle the German language, imploding the prestige of Germanity. The foreign agents lodged in the heart of the nation must be expelled, for "German must be *protected* and immunized against any contamination, especially one coming from within, through fake Germans who do not speak true German and whom we should eliminate as soon as possible."[21] The traffickers of a fake German ID are viewed as dead or phantom foreigners, invaders who have been set on Germanity largely to corrupt the language. There are many twists, including those from which Fichte's argument takes off, that consolidate his concerns with

assuring freedom and the necessity of commit-
ting to a *cosmopolitan* expanse. This paradoxical
climb may seem difficult to disentangle today,
but let us not forget that "freedom fighters"
and those who ride the signifier of liberty to
the ground come from one of the speculative
tracks that brandish freedom – a hard-hitting
Schlagwort that can be retrieved by right-wing
and religious formations as well as by ardent
seekers of social justice.

*****

Admittedly I've tolerated a number of logical
leaps in order to place the discussion of America
and "America" – a material and historical field of
superseded meaning as country and dream logic,
doubled by its European partner in disjointure
and speculative figuration. This linkage may earn
me a yellow card, because the prime counterpart
in Germany – the taunts, the desperate rounds
of self-inflation – were played out mainly in
philosophical precincts, providing premises for
empirical markers attended by barely containable
historical narratives and runaway myths in the
form of nationalist fiction.

So. Have we landed anywhere, or is it time to switch on "Ground Control to Major Tom"? Yes and no. We don't know where "love of country" comes from, what kinds of sublimations and distortions it entails, but we know where it leads and the renunciations required by maturity. Goethe tried to refute nationalist or land-based claims with the antiballistic shield of *Weltliteratur* (world literature) and other forms of worlding that are resistant to provincial forms of patriotism and referential bordering. How does all this land in us today?

We still need to dig in to know what *land* is, a configuration of *Ort* (place) and embedded *Erörterung* that makes room for notions of conquest in historically assignable territories and their unconscious domestications. Adherence to country has puzzled Shakespeare as much as Lacan, repelled Emerson as much as Nietzsche, tormented Wittgenstein as well as James Baldwin. In Shakespeare, Fortinbras notes that the Hamlet brood crashed to its downfall over an inch of land. What propels subjects, he muses, to accept the terms of *dying for* their country? Lacan argues that the thirst for Lebensraum, a nationalized craving for extension, is stronger even than the death drive. Both Shakespeare and Lacan, among other psychoanalytic transmitters, understood the feminine silhouette that invests the very notion of *country*, going so far as to motivate the incessant drive to protect (or bomb) a heavily symbolized territory of the maternal empire. A boundarized country is not solely tethered to philosophical and material forms of viability, but its imaginary field spills over, cajoles, retracts, and informs the self-comprehension of the nation state in its mutability. Yet something as minute as a slogan can inflect or sabotage the way a country conceives of itself, receives notice of its usable imago, and runs with a disabling fiction of nationhood. In each case, or am I dreaming, philosophical precepts format and arrange for the practice of a nation's diverse inscriptions, framing the way remembrance or effacement are practiced and injury apportioned. Let us return to homebase in *Heimat* (homeland) fashioning, to look at what persists in structuring our principal political stances, often covertly maintained.

Still (and always), one cannot simply conflate Heidegger with Fichte, even when they appear to share the same referential and politically calibrated field. Fichte's recourse to an *Urvolk*, a primal

or arch people, does not bear the same consequence as Heidegger's convocation of *Germania*.
Ahead of the curve, Fichte assembles forces that
override the premium of national frontiers and
narcissistically limiting concerns: following a different game plan, he's better than that. Here's
how. Fichte aims the gains made by the arch
people at the entirety of humanity, sidelining
those who are *engherzich*, narrow-hearted and
hostile to others, phobic about foreign incursions
– if one can even locate what is foreign, exter-
nal, and foreboding. Motivated by the thought of
ennobling and by universalist goals, these volks,
promoted by Fichte, evolve through the *cosmopo-
litical task of science and language* when making
their pitches for a self-transcending humanity.
There was no Germany, and thus no "German"
idealism when Fichte was going after a credible
syntagm of patriotism. He was looking at what
makes the *opposite* of a strictly nationalist bend.[22]
German patriotism, organized around the directives of scientific probity (also a Nietzschean
theme) and language (ditto), was resolutely carried out on behalf of the *Menschengeschlecht*, the
human species, blowing off many of the markers we associate with the limiting count-offs of

a nation state. Hence Peter Trawny's emphasis on an idiomatic and idiotic self-assertion, which designates no more than a vapid bodying forth of the bodiless nation. Fichte delineates the conditions for creating a *cosmopolitan patriot*, which almost means a Jewish–Kantian–Moses Mendelssohnian patriotism, even where a craving shows up for a universal topos supplemented by concessions to materially mapped land markers. Heidegger picks up the charge and runs it in a different direction, letting "land" in Trakl shade into *Abendland* (evening land, occident), marking the spot where the West moves into ideological sunset.

*****

The harshest criticism can, and *must*, accrue to the culture that invented critique and left off, embarking on a destructive adventure to establish and mystify its legacy. Scanning the onto-semantic hold of *Geschlecht*, Heidegger and Derrida conceive of historical denting, branding, and forms of identification in terms of *hits*, including the metaphysical strike that sears gender. Exactly how we are struck matters, though Heidegger and Derrida handle these strikes differently. Just as there are bad hits, or the off-target and badly misfiring *envois* and *Schläge* – the slams of the kind Heidegger describes – there's a stain in and of *Geschlecht* that Heidegger, riding Trakl, tries to wrestle, obliquely stressing what is *schlecht* (bad) in *Geschlecht*. We are fated to be struck – but also to hit bottom, sidelined and wrongly addressed – as a form of taking historical shape.

*****

In *Geschlecht III* and a number of related build-ups, Derrida considers yet another aspect of the long haul of Germanic philosophical self-affirmation and confident superiority, binding a vexed tradition to which we continue to bear witness and make appropriative runs. Even those cleared of suspicion in applications of persecuting frames, exilic warriors who might be exempted from excesses of national–speculative pride, have fallen in line with an aspect of Fichte's argument, embracing the temptation to redeem some unconscious follow-through on the prerogatives of appointed or phantasmatic nationhood. From early on, missile-guided by

Fichte from a different time zone, Germanity would henceforth offer itself superior test results as a national–philosophical power base. Few escape the requital of covert anointment. Thus political and cultural theorists of unquestionable courage and refinement have tended to adopt, at some level of awareness, a superior sense of adherence to a surviving Weltbild, a German philosophical grounding compatible with that of Fichte & Co. You cannot tell me that even world-class renegades supplied with intellectual rigor and autonomy, for example Werner Hamacher and Jacob Taubes (to take a swath of aboveboard contestants), did not take a hit of German pride with their deracination. Germanity, no matter how decisively distilled to a minor essence, may still be on tap as the witches' brew. We can always test out the revival of a provocative Germanity. [§Sidebar] Along with brutal expulsions and pariah markdowns, the coerced transitions and trials of self-alienating translation work of the twentieth century, Arendt, Adorno, Thomas Mann, Schoenberg, and other transplants in America implicitly adhered to such a view, evincing a feeling tone that attests to the leading role assumed by the German language in vital matters of thought and poesy. One of the few holdouts may be Reiner

Schürmann, who refused the German language – a type or species of refusal that, transposed to my own family history, gave the rejected language wound only a stronger hold. In terms of a more popular and equally abiding cultural screenshot, my parents stood with Marlene Dietrich. . . . *Enter Angela Merkel.* Queasily accommodating herself to the craft of diplomacy in the twenty-first century, she listens to Trump saying to her that he in fact is a German. *Eyeroll, breathwork; her mouth distorts.* Once upon a time: we were one *Geschlecht.* Struck apart, a curse. [*StopSidebar*]

*****

Holy *Unfug*! Two calls made Trumpf impeachment-ready. A tangle of calls on January 6, a few declined, he refuses to call off his dogs. Let us patch these flash calls through to our switchboard, remembering how telephony, a chip of *Gestell*, situates the technologically constellated state. Freud, Heidegger, Derrida – and "America" – were trained on the telephone, each in a singular way sending electronic signals, recovering calls on a storage machine of latency or, indeed, stocking messages of historical urgency, structured by a call-forwarding system that still pulsates today.

Having covered some of these motifs, I do not want to retrace the calls taken by Heidegger or the ones, rerouted through Freud, declined by Derrida. Or even pick up on Nietzsche's telephone to the beyond, when installing Dionysus. Let us simply bring the political facticity of a recent batch of calls into sonic view and critical viability. Trumpf made two calls that he assessed as "perfect calls" – an assessment that, from his perspective, did not have to scour for meaning or establish a semanticized solidity: yes, maybe, "perfect" calls, bully calls, threatening calls, dial M for murder calls, aphonic calls, invasive and crushing, on the take. This is not far from the nexus that sets up the call of conscience in the vicinity of technology, unavoidably part of a mug for criminal infraction. Perhaps it is a small irony that technology also shut him down at the end of that session, putting a part-time cross on the Twitter account that sustained his power and invasive demands in the first round of injurious governance. Trumpf's reliance on technopathologies (including the positive technics of television, telephone, and social media and the associated rejection of medical science) retries, for us, *The Question Concerning Technology*, giving the character of technological intimidation the upper hand, a means to throttling adversity, delivering death threats, or calling in favors. Trumpf could be hung by the umbilicus of his telephone, an old-fashioned model for intrusive power plugs on which he, like Stalin and other old-school tyrannical soul structures, depended for his pointed shoot-outs.

As Trumpf lumbers in and out of the presidency, one counts down the retreat and returns of an anti-democratic team supercharged by masculinist pathologies that bear for us the imprint of a protest gone bad – struck, in terms of Nietzschean evaluation, by a radically decadent and pessimistic imprint. Trumpf, a pit of grievance unbounded, is the sign of a protest gone "bad, very bad," in his retributive locution. The name, refitted with the missing "f," rings with one that Thomas Mann, or Flaubert before him, could write into a narrative that seeks to capture mediocrity by naming and a promiscuous capacity for full-scale wreckage. One wonders, when asked to induce the pressures of critique and melancholic distress: how did this come about on our watch? What characterizes the back-alley return of overblown Germanity at a time of scientific maturity allotted for inhabiting this earth – our time, divided and regressed, attended by a particular stopwatch that checks periodically on Being and nihilism, signaling a new storm surge that upends hard-won values of "cosmopolitan" regulatory ideals? Of course, these values and the purported maturity that subtends them have been submitted to relentless critique, even as they profess a glimmer of progressive enlightenment.

The tireless reach of a past falsely resolved is menacing by necessity, spills into the way we move or stagger through darkened fields of political comprehension. Together with the increase in extremist types of stand-down, figures of Nazism keep returning in the extended western world, as if on automatic replay, citing the traumatism of a repetition compulsion inflated to historical proportions. Groups ranging from Proud Boys to Oath Keepers, Sovereign Citizens, and other members of born-again fascism have brandished Nazi–American emblems and T-shirts Camp Auschwitz and 6MWNE ("six million was not enough") – the newer version of what Lacan would call a "symptax," a class of unspeakable injuries that tie wide-ranging American depravity to the German example, ineffaceable and ready to roll out on the cusp of metaphysical self-determination.

What now?

Ethical anxiety leaves us hanging, and remains as intractable as the origin of Kant's categorical imperative: from whom (or what) shall we take our cues, heed orders – whether these be formulated as marching orders, in the name of social justice or orders to halt, or given in terms of recommitting to a puffed-up sense of world, as it widely "unworlds" to the beat of a Freudian *Aggressionstrieb*, maintaining a calamitous regression to state-owned narcissistic violence? Under the sway of what or whom does one feel justly prodded, shaken down by claims of justice from the future? To be sure, there are false calls that enjoin us to answer, on trend and superficial, but also genuine assignments, urging that one become rigorously heedful, whether motivated or immobilized, temporarily deprogrammed, set for action, benched, ideologically retrofitted, hit or *verschlagen* (knocked off course), off balance, prepared or not for a retest, or theoretically frozen in place, desperately waiting for a sign.

Given access to a longer runway, I would want to prepare another batch of Derrida's exacting motifs for consideration at this time. It should include the reflections on seizures of statehood in the Middle East, or the pressure put on us by Trumpf's work on the death penalty – a live American wire – in the form of an unprecedented acceleration of executions on the eve of his departure from office. Or the way in which the very thought of the gift of forgiveness, framing acts of pardon, has risen to the level of political apprehension in the United States, as a few years ago the outgoing president indulged in an orgy of pardons, implicating the pervertibility of forgiveness in the warp of self-pardon, with all its metaphysical requisites – which entailed acts of public declaration, vow, oath, precedent, contract law, date, and signature.

One would need, moreover, to see at this time how *testing* works not only in terms of resetting political norms and limits, but by focusing the comorbidities that stick to aggressive forms of Trumpfism – for instance in the drama, still potent, around the nearly unchecked viral rampage and in the ongoing fight, religiously boosted, over scientific probity and trials, evidentiary standards, and methods of truth assertion. How has testing enabled a structuring, if ironically posited, in relation to the memory of a world fragment we still aspire to support and share? How are we *timed* by the shift to newer modalities of testing, initiated in part by Nietzsche's "Americanny" observations that refine an experimental disposition, subjected to incessant testing, and its American – canny, uncanny – counterparts? How do we stand and understand the test of time, the proving grounds of the untimely, the Nietzschean cadence, our time out, or time immemorial clocked at different checkpoints in our being-in-common? One pauses over the poets – and phantoms – whose insomniac exertions cover the night shift of philosophical questioning.

What time is it? Tuned by Arendt to the darkest times and by Hamacher to the arrest of time after Auschwitz, staggered by the rule of revenants, flashbacks, mythical retrievals, regressive stalls, and traumatic blankouts, one would need rigorously to consider the differing flowcharts of time in Heidegger and Derrida – waves of granting, types of favoring, the beat of poetic donation, the ticking menace of denials, and instabilities of and in time set between moments, undecidably given as trace. On another beat, one would also be drawn to heed the figuring of modalities of time given as indeterminacy (*archē*, lapse, moment, *eschaton*, duration, present, suspension, telos, rhythm, hurried instances, diachrony, the rush of ecstatic temporality, an *Augenblick*, and other tics and tocs, the beat of Madame "de Maintenant," given time, the many times and climes that declares, "Your time is up," repetition compulsion, down for the count, etc., etc.).[23]

Clearly, the larger cast of these questions must be engaged elsewhere, connecting to time zones that account for history set apart from historial time, the difference in Heidegger between *Historie* and *Geschichte*. In the meantime, and for the duration, one is out there, voided, ghosted, twisting in the air, stirred listlessly, abandoned to our abandonment, shaken by the pathos of co-responsiveness without address. *Ouf.* It could well be that, on appeased days, one is oddly picked up by the thrall of being-toward-death, another beatdown, a strangely refreshing wounding that lifts according to the stroke or *Schlag* of another timekeeper.

Ach! Keeping with the stabs of unworlding, let me call it a day. Tomorrow I will rise up differently. (Or so she thought.)

Notes

Notes to Part 1

1 Philippe Lacoue-Labarthe, *Heidegger and the Politics of Poetry* (Urbana: University of Illinois Press, 2007), p. 68.

2 Alenka Zupančič, "The Chorus and the Real in Poetic Art" (2011), lecture delivered at the European Graduate School in Switzerland. https://egs.edu/lecture/alenka-zupancic-the-chorus-and-the-real-in-poetic-art-2011.

3 Alanna Nash, *The Colonel* (New York: Simon & Schuster, 2010), p. 177.

4 Stanley Cavell, *This New yet Unapproachable America: Lectures after Emerson after Wittgenstein* (Albuquerque, New Mexico: Living Batch Press, 1989), p. 92. See on this the analysis of Isabelle Alfandary, "Unfounding an American Tradition: Or the Performative Invention of Self in Ralph Waldo Emerson" (2019). Textual Practice 33.10. https://www.tandfonline.com/doi/full/10.1080/0950236X.2019.1665924.

5 Cavell, *This New yet Unapproachable America*, p. 92.
6 Ibid., p. 95.
7 Lacoue-Labarthe, *Heidegger*, p. 12.
8 Martin Heidegger, "The Origin of the Work of Art," as quoted in Lacoue-Labarthe, *Heidegger*, p. 12.
9 Cavell, *This New yet Unapproachable America*, p. 69.
10 Ibid., p. 70.
11 Ibid.
12 Ibid., p. 71.
13 Ibid., p. 72.
14 Jacques Derrida, "FORS," translated by Barbara Johnson. *Georgia Review* 31.1 (1977): 64–116.
15 Cavell, *This New yet Unapproachable America*, p. 71.
16 Ibid. (quoting from Rush Rees ed., *Recollections of Wittgenstein*).
17 Ibid., pp. 71 and 72.
18 Ibid., p. 84.
19 Ibid.
20 Ibid., p. 85.
21 Ibid.
22 Ibid.
23 Ibid., p. 73.
24 Ibid., p. 93.
25 Ibid., p. 74.

Notes to Part 2

1 In Hölderlin and Heidegger, *Unfug* (roguery, mischief) refers to a serious frivolity, a trespass against the gods.
2 Heidegger's intrusion upon the political scene, a relentless tendency in which he superseded all other

philosophers who preceded him, including Plato, is a point hammered home by Jean-Luc Nancy in a number of works.

3 Rainer Maria Rilke, *Duineser Elegien* I (Berlin: Suhrkamp, 1994).

4 Jacques Derrida, *Rogues: Two Essays on Reason*, translated by Pascale-Anne Brault and Michael Naas (Stanford, CA: Stanford University Press, 2005), p. 37.

5 Ibid., p. 40.

6 The English title, *What Is Philosophy?* pares down the verve of Heidegger's original title, which is that of a lecture: "Was ist das – die Philosophie?" First delivered in Cerisy-la-Salle, Normandy, in 1955, this lecture was meant *zur Einleitung eines Gesprächs* ("to introduce a discussion"). It interrogates the *Washeit* – "whatness" – of essential philosophical questioning. In this text Heidegger situates genuine philosophy as *Gespräch*. He explicitly downgrades the Latinate *Konversation* – "conversation" – to the level of "the unphilosophical." Bearing the address and the place (*Ort*), Normandy, in mind, one can imagine what the French in conversation with Heidegger – driven there, to Cerisy, with Elfriede Heidegger, by a speeding Lacan – had to swallow. Upon disembarking, Elfriede, in appreciation of Nazi engineering, exclaimed: "We built you good roads! *Was ist das –* ? ['What is this – ?']." What was said at Cerisy by Madame Heidegger has been verified by Marguerite Derrida and Maurice de Gandillac, the director of Cerisy-la-Salle.

7 An analysis of Heidegger's self-asserted "dumbest" move can be found in Avital Ronell, *Stupidity* (Chicago: University of Illinois Press, 2002).

8 See Kaplan's discussion of Rilke's disparagement of a "repugnant" America that "he knew practically nothing about": Steven Kaplan, "Modern American Poets on Rilke's 'Things' and Robert Bly as a Translator of Rilke's Images and Objects." *Translation Review* 38/39.1 (1992): 66–71. DOI: 10.1080/07374836.1992.10523541.

9 Nicolaus Lenau, *Sämtliche Werke*, edited by Anastasius Grün (Stuttgart: J. G. Cotta, 1855), vol. 2. OK. Lenau, *nom de plume* for Nikolaus Franz Niembsch Edler von Strehlenau, actually experienced America. He migrated from Habsburg to Baltimore and Ohio, where he felt he was condemned forever to be stuck in dreary desolation.

10 I am tempted to invoke the feminine usage of the term "metaphysics" (which German shares with Romance languages) as part of an autobiographical trace. In *The Post Card* Derrida describes our initial meeting, an overwrought scene at a time when I introduced myself as Metaphysics (*la Métaphysique*). To this day some people call me by my other name, Metaphysics, or, depending on my itinerary, *la Métaphysique* and even *die Metaphysik*. See "Le 23 juin 1979" and "Le 21 août 1979" in "Envois," in Jacques Derrida, *La Carte Postale: De Socrate à Freud et au-delà* (Paris: Flammarion, 1980), pp. 211–13 and pp. 262–3.

11 This is a theme discussed in Noam Chomsky's well-known interviews on the betrayals and innate failures of America's democratic institutions. At another level of egregiously compromised integrity, slaveowners where pitching for freedom, a point of grossly hypocritical contention that riled the Europeans – as, for example, when Phillis Wheatley, the mother of African American

poetry, was showcased in London by her "enlightened" owners. Aristocratic members of the abolitionist movement in England wondered why those who revered her talent did not free her. Wheatley was long disavowed or left for undead in American Black poetry anthologies, and suffered a list of tragic indignities when she was let loose and married.

12 I discuss the nature of nationalized test sites and their theological substructures in Avital Ronell, *The Test Drive* (Chicago: University of Illinois Press, 2007). A first-round analysis of Heidegger's attack on America appears in Avital Ronell, "The Gestell from Hell: Philosophy Sets Up 'America.'" *Oxford Literary Review* 43.1 (2021; special issue "A Conversation with Jacques Derrida about Heidegger," edited by Rodrigo Therezo and Geoffrey Bennington): 107–30.

13 Sarah Kofman, *Séductions: De Sartre à Héraclite* (Paris: Galilée, 1990).

14 Philippe Lacoue-Labarthe, *Phrases* (Paris: Christian Bourgois, 1990).

15 See especially the commentary of on Heideggerian tropes of unity in Richard Beardsworth, *Derrida and the Political* (London: Routledge, 1990), p. III.

16 Strangely disavowed but still pumping, something returns to America from Germanic roots and boots, and the rhetoric of unconscious tactical maneuvers must not be left out of a picture that assumes the false allure of transparency. See Laurence Rickels, *Germany: A Science Fiction* (Fort Wayne, IN: Anti-Oedipus Press, 2015). It is also worth mentioning here Friedrich Kittler's massive cathexis, in various studies of Thomas Pynchon's novels,

on the German American lines consistently drawn in those novels.

17 Jacques Derrida, "Declarations of Independence," in his *Negotiations*, edited by Elizabeth Rottenberg (Stanford, CA: Stanford University Press, 2002).

18 Hélène Cixous, "Jacques Derrida: Co-Responding Voix You," in *Derrida and the Time of the Political*, edited by Suzanne Guerlac and Pheng Cheah (Durham, NC: Duke University Press, 2009), p. 46.

19 Jacques Derrida, *Geschlecht III: Sexe, race, nation, humanité*, edited by Geoffrey Bennington, Katie Chenoweth, and Rodrigo Therezon (Paris: Seuil, 2018), p. 25.

20 Ibid., p. 21: "[I]l faut *garder* l'allemand et l'immuniser contre toute contamination, surtout si elle vient du dedans à travers les faux Allemands qui ne parlent pas le vrai allemand et dont il faudrait se débarraser aussitôt que possible."

21 Ibid., p. 23.

22 Peter Trawny has given an analysis of the perversion of "patriotism" in a paper delivered at the "Geschlecht III" Conference organized by Katie Chenwith and Rodrigo Therezo, Princeton University, 2018.

23 Beyond expanded timetables ticking down on hollow times, bad timing, the empty interval, dead zones, and ghostly returns, one needs to return to the temporal spark of the *Augenblick*, "instant or blink of an eye," which is cast with acuity in Geoffrey Bennington, *Scatter 1: The Politics of Politics in Foucault, Heidegger, and Derrida* (New York: Fordham University Press, 2016).